HEALTHY DISRUPTION

The Benefit and Burden
of A Black Healthcare
Executive in America

HEALTHY DISRUPTION

The Benefit and Burden of A Black Healthcare Executive in America

GYASI C. CHISLEY

Healthy Disruption

Gyasi C. Chisley

Copyright 2021

Printed in the United States of America.

All Rights Reserved.

No part of this work may be reproduced or transmitted in any form or by any means, electronic or mechanical, including photocopying and recording, or by any information storage or retrieval system, except as may be expressly permitted by the 1976 Copyright Act or in writing from the publisher.

ISBN: 9-781-0880-0434-0

Foreword

True disruption rarely ever occurs, yet it is the thing that allows for radical change if we choose to lean into uncomfortable spaces and try incredibly different things. Why do different things? We all know the quote about insanity: "Doing the same thing over and over again and expecting different results." *Healthy Disruption: The Benefit and Burden of a Black Healthcare Executive in America* is how author Gyasi Chisley helps us understand how we can disrupt the status quo of the American healthcare system and create something that works. To do this, however, we must try different approaches and solutions.

I grew up in New York City, the largest microcosm of this country. One of the ways I learned about life was through the lens of driving taxi cabs during a summer college break. My first postgraduate school hospital administration job was as an emergency department administrator. EDs are the largest microcosm of health care and serve as the gateway between the hospital and what happens out in society each day. I retired as CEO of CommonSpirit Health, one of the largest health systems in the nation. Spanning 21 states and serving cities as large as Los Angeles and Houston, as well as small rural communities like Devil's Lake, North Dakota, and Garden City, Kansas, CommonSpirit is a microcosm of health care in America. These experiences give me a deep and broad lens on US health care. My experiences also confirm that health care remains a broken, inequitable system.

This book could not be timelier and is on-point to help us act on a promise yet to be fulfilled. *Crossing the Quality Chasm*, the groundbreaking research published by the Institutes of Medicine in 2001, clearly documented that a disparity in healthcare access, treatment, and outcome existed when comparing care between Black and White people in this country. Yet, 20 years later, the COVID-19 pandemic once again highlighted these same disparities and made it worse. Why? What was done over two decades to try to change it? This is insanity at its best! One thing is certain: The pandemic was a disruptor. Many things will never be the same. However, as a society, are we using the pandemic to make things better? Will we make health care better in our country?

The political and social climate in the country has only made the task of improving the health status for all more difficult. If anything, the last couple of years allowed for "unhealthy" disruption. Despite the high-profile cases of police killing unarmed Blacks in the street or in their homes, blatant, in-your-face racism in America was allowed to resurface in a way our country had not seen since the 1960s.

People who work in health care must strive for social justice and equality in how we help care for people. Patients come to us when they are most vulnerable, when they are sick or injured. However, many in the general population would roll back the clock to the days of Jim Crow. They contrive other ways to discount or hold back people of color. They use voter suppression to maintain control of politics, withhold vaccines, and do not follow proper public health guidelines to maintain a superiority in health status.

While we keep changing the labels—affirmative action to diversity; now to diversity, equity, and inclusion—the results stay the same. Why? Changing the label may help people leading organizations feel better, but it does not change anything. I cannot count the number of times in my career that I was the first or only Black healthcare executive to do this or to do that. For example, at one time, Percy Allen and I were the only two Black CEOs leading university hospitals in this country. Today, there is only one. Why is it that 43 years after my career began, a brilliant, next-generation leader like Gyasi Chisley is still dealing with many of the same issues people that my generation dealt with?

By tackling these uncomfortable topics, this book helps us understand the issues behind the issues. If we courageously use the information and learnings within these chapters, it will help us develop good, sustainable solutions and make meaningful, long-lasting change.

I love the way Gyasi embedded concepts around health and healthy choices into every chapter of the book. The quality of life people enjoy is directly related to the quality of their health. The quality of their health is disproportionately affected by the social determinants of health (SDOH). The SDOH are directly affected by where people live, learn, work, and play. Having healthcare leaders who have experience—or at least can better understand, empathize, and communicate with people like themselves—is a critical factor of success when improving the health of people and communities.

Throughout my career, by being "in the room where it happens" (a lyric from the Broadway play *Hamilton*), I was in a position and chose to speak up, offer a diverse position or point of view, and improve the decision or outcome we were addressing. The only way that occurs is to have leaders with diverse backgrounds and experiences at the top, on the board, and "in the room."

I am proud that Gyasi would call me his mentor, a person he learns from and listens to, but it is reciprocal. I am learning from and listening to his perspectives of our healthcare system through *Healthy Disruptions*. He is mentoring me. By reading this book, he is challenging us to become disruptive leaders. It is healthy to be disruptive for positive change. Just do it!

    Kevin E. Lofton, LFACHE
    CEO Emeritus
    CommonSpiritHealth

Contents

Foreword 5

Introduction 11
Developing a Healthy Perspective

Chapter 1 23
*Working to Establish a Healthy Family
in an Unhealthy Environment*

Chapter 2 43
*Building Healthy Communities
for Real Equity*

Chapter 3 67
*A Healthy Assessment of the Pandemic,
the Protests, and the Loss of Profit
Within Health Care and Throughout the United States*

Chapter 4 91
Creating a Healthy Platform for Change

Chapter 5 109
Leadership in Unhealthy Times

Chapter 6 125
Finding the Way Forward to a Healthy Future

Epilogue 139
*The Healthy Connection Between Compassion,
Empathy, and Disruption*

Dedication

FOR my hero: Marley Milan Jeannette Chisley

TO my family: the Chisleys, Haddixes, Keenons, Atkinses, Cunnighams, Galbreaths, and Washingtons

WITH my people: the disenfranchised and the voiceless

BECAUSE it is time to confront and disrupt the standard that has plagued us for generations

BY the grace and mercy of God and the Universe

I am because WE are.

Introduction

Developing a Healthy Perspective

"I'm clear why I'm here. How 'bout you?" Jay-Z

There is a lot of pain in this country and within the healthcare industry. The state of a divided republic and the broken healthcare system are inextricably tied and should not only be called out, but should be examined and overhauled to achieve a better country and industry.

In 2020, the healthcare system's fragility was exposed. The disparities and access issues were highlighted by the pandemic, but the racial injustice that America continues to ignore from slavery to Jim Crow to murder served as a mirror that America could no longer ignore. The pandemic exacerbated all of America's inconsistencies, such as "all men are created equal" (underlying the fact that Black people, women, and minorities are also "citizens" and that the concept of equality often does not apply).

HEALTHY DISRUPTION

The year further uncovered the fact that America's kick-the-can-down-the-road mentality ultimately comes back to bite her in the ass in a major way. This is most evident when the privileged flaunt what they have achieved through schemes and loopholes that the underprivileged do not have access to and when everyone, due to the pandemic quarantine mandates, is glued to their respective devices watching America look at its ugliness in the mirror in real time.

If you have ever imbibed too many spirits in a specific time frame, you have experienced the effects of a hangover. Collectively, we will be experiencing the hangover effects of 2020 for many years to come. This country, as well as the healthcare industry (because they are so interconnected), will stomach the hangover effect differently and shoulder a burden to change system, processes, and people or face the strong possibility of becoming irrelevant.

Moreover, Black people in this country and in leading healthcare institutions will have to confront the aftermath of this past year and will have to be strategically decisive on how to navigate the country and the industry. The 3 P's of the last year cemented who we are. Now we must decide who we will become in health care and throughout the country.

- Pandemic
- Protests
- Profit

The pandemic disproportionately impacted underprivileged communities and Black people more than any other race. The murders of Ahmaud Arbery, Breonna Taylor, and George Floyd (unfortunately, to name only a few) and protests that ensued unfolded because the privileged saw almost in real time what Black people have known

INTRODUCTION

for years: "It is more dangerous to be Black in this country than white," said Tim Walz, governor of Minnesota. Even with going from dumb ass to kick ass in the White House, the last P is in full effect.

This past year, the wealth gap widened by nearly 20 percent for white families and over 40 percent for Black families.[1] This chasm has led to greater inequality as higher education and health screenings were delayed due to financial hardships, especially within communities of color.

Some people might write off these facts as coincidences. If you are like me and subscribe to everything being tied to health in this country, then you know that America manufactures everything for her benefit. In a capitalistic society like America, profit is always the determining factor, and the other two P's (pandemic and protests) are viewed as opportunities to make more money for the privileged.

Most of this information is probably well-known to the reader, nothing new. However, the oxymoronic title of this project, *Healthy Disruption*, is based on the premise that *everything* is related to health in this country and that, in one way or another, we are all in the business of health care. We will examine and work to prove this fact throughout the text.

While everything is related to health, health and health care are two distinct concepts. *Health* has everything to do with a person's environs, access, and education; while *health care* is a business like any other endeavor in America, aimed at profit, with little to no mission or altruism tied to it.

Big Pharma comprises most of the major pharmaceutical companies, such as Merck, AstraZeneca, Pfizer, and Johnson & Johnson. Payers include large insurance companies, such as UnitedHealthcare,

HEALTHY DISRUPTION

Blue Cross/Blue Shield, Cigna, Aetna, and Humana. Together, Big Pharma and payers make most healthcare delivery almost exclusively "hospital-centric" because it is more profitable for both healthcare entities.

Hedge funds (net premiums in 2019 were $1.3 trillion) paid vendors and consulting firms $12 billion in 2019.[2] Hedge funds make public bets on big companies such as Big Pharma and other payers, and the healthcare industry has often been the target of hedge funds that can increase or decrease the value of companies that make many of the products within health care. Thus, they increase the cost back to the consumer.

However, when we look more closely at what consumers are paying for, we see that waste and unnecessary services were estimated last year to be between $760 billion to $935 billion.[3] Meanwhile, private equity and venture capital firms infused nearly $41 billion in last quarter, with expectations to rectify an industry that has been repaired, revisited, revised, and reregulated.[4]

This past year underscored that, in many ways, most Black and underprivileged communities do not have access to health care. A person's zip code has far more to do with health and determinants of life expectancy than that person's genetic code. As my beloved advisor Bernard J. Tyson (Rest in Power) would say, "Your health is your wealth." This project is intended to help the reader identify this very fact. The purpose is to road map opportunities to disrupt not only the healthcare industry, but a country that relies on an industry that comprises a "healthy" fraction of the economy.

In 2020, the country and the healthcare industry were almost broken without recourse for repair—and so was I. I was on the brink of despair for a country I love that does not love me back and for an

INTRODUCTION

industry to which I have devoted myself but has not shown the same level of commitment to me. I was emoting, and I was angry at the state of affairs and everything that emanated from the 3 P's, particularly the pandemic and the protests. It was a cry for help as the lingering effects of the pandemic and the murders of Black people at the hands of authorities persisted. My anger turned into this initiative. As Chuck D from Public Enemy once said, "When I get mad, I put down on a pad, give you something that you never had."

As I was being called the n-word for proliferating and promoting Black pride, Black struggle, and Black emotion in a predominantly white company, country, and industry with earmark celebrations such as Juneteenth, I started my soul search inward. My self-diagnosis was threefold:

1. I was more anxious than ever. Throughout my career, I have had what some would call success, but that success brought with it a constant fear of losing it, fear of the police, and fear that I would lose it and be penalized for it. I am exponentially more anxious now than when I was broke and had nothing. With George Floyd being the modern-day Emmett Till, my anxiety was brought on by the state of affairs within this country. In the healthcare industry—which is insular, primarily run by white men, and serves the privileged differently from the underserved—my anxiety was only intensified.

2. I, like many Black people, suffer from two chronic diseases that should be eradicated from our psyche: survivors' remorse/guilt and the "disease to please." For most Black people, particularly in leadership roles, these diseases are prevalent, and they eat at the core of our mental stability as

well as erode our opportunities to build, find, and sustain empowerment. Speaking from experience, I see the effects manifest themselves among Black leaders within health care nearly every day.

3. Therefore, the conclusion is that I am complicit in the issue. My self-reflection took me through a journey of my childhood and my family on a journey of journaling the juxtaposition of the healthcare industry and how it serves as a microcosm of America in the worst ways. Then, finally, I was able to devise lasting solutions to address the ills and chasms.

This journey required an unquenched thirst for information and outreach. Within the information-building phase of my journey, it dawned on me that humans have the need for three things: (1) to be validated, (2) to contribute, and (3) to be relevant. All of these human necessities proved difficult to achieve during the height of the pandemic. However, the second phase in my outreach to others was deliberate, and I was working hard to understand different perspectives and glean further insights into my aforementioned self-diagnosis.

Much to my dismay, after speaking with many of my colleagues, friends, and family members, I came to the conclusion that the need for and ability to change in this country and throughout the healthcare industry is not only real, but palpable. The adage "Everyone says they want change until it happens to them" was apparent in me and in other people I had spoken with. Dr. Jack Cox, a good friend of mine, struck a cautionary note when he said, "If you don't like change, you're going to like irrelevance even less." I also learned

INTRODUCTION

that many leaders, especially within health care, do not view leadership as a choice and have forgotten (or never knew) that passion over position serves the greater good to a wayward industry and a wayward country losing its way.

The opportunity to capture triumph over tragedy can only be harnessed through empathy in the industry and throughout the country. My epiphany surrounding white leaders in the industry is not that white people necessarily lack empathy. It is more so that they do not know how to empathize. More to my disbelief and chagrin, Black leaders have adopted the sentiment not to display empathy or they have deeply suppressed it, which goes against most natural tendencies of Black people.

While conducting interviews, I also worked to evangelize, incorporate, and rediscover the growth mindset. I was saddened that health care—and this country, for that matter—lack big ideas and the acumen to try to execute an obvious concept that has been in the ether for decades, regardless of the healthcare sector (provider, payer, or pharma, for example).

However, it is not all doom and gloom. I was thoroughly encouraged that there is a rising shared consciousness, particularly among younger generations, that features the growth mindset in most of their thought processes as they challenge the status quo. Over the last year, we have seen their uncanny ability to mobilize in the wake of the social injustice within our country. I am predicting that health care will be next to be disrupted—intentionally by courageous leadership or unintentionally from outsiders to the industry.

Those within the healthcare industry tend to be unable to unlearn certain perspectives and theories that many have written about, lectured on, and regurgitated in the past on how to fix health care. This

HEALTHY DISRUPTION

is particularly true and exhibited by the privileged and traditional leadership in health care, as well as in America.

Moreover, Black leaders have a pivotal opportunity—even a responsibility—to seize this moment, create momentum, and start a movement to fundamentally change health care and America. Black people, especially Black leaders, are uniquely equipped for this moment. All of the unfortunate and unnecessary anguish, anxiety, and acceptance of injustice in this country has uniquely prepared and manufactured a strong spirituality and relatability factor that today's leaders need now more than ever. In my mind, relatability and relevance are interconnected.

Black people, when demonstrating true authenticity in the workplace and in circles throughout this country, can relate to other people's trials, tribulations, and triumphs like no other race. Thus, as an offshoot of the country, the same can be said for health care. Leaders and those who have devoted their life's work to the industry have continuously resuscitated the goal to be altruistic and an economic engine simultaneously. Health care can be the industry that personifies the American dream, emblematic of the maxim "When you do go, you can also do well."

In addition, there is a lot of what the artist Drake would call "fake love" surrounding the need for diversity, equity, and inclusion. However, it often lacks substance, capital, and skill set to revolutionize a stale concept in many Fortune 500 companies, as well as the entire healthcare industry.

I have never been around a more creative people than Black people, but we have not been empowered in the past to express that creativity nor bring our whole selves, the best versions of who we are and what we represent, to the table. This moment was built for

INTRODUCTION

us, and we should put the growth mindset top of mind and begin to execute toward a more empowered future. After all, our DNA and philosophy can be traced back to Africa from the concept and spirit of *Ubuntu*.

Originally, I wanted to call this project *Ubuntu*, but I did not want to lose focus on our opportunity to address the state of this country and the healthcare industry. *Ubuntu* can be summarized as "I am because we are." Unlike traditional capitalism, *Ubuntu* focuses on the need to enlarge the proverbial pie and guards against the approach of slicing it further, particularly when the slicing benefits the privileged, those who already possess a large portion of the pie.

The solutions, which we will explore in this text, are found when enlightened leaders solve for the 7 C's:

- Culture
- Consolidation
- Commercialization
- Consumerism
- Coalition-building
- Concept-to-execution
- Control

Through my interviews and research, there is an ongoing campaign to protect the privileged. However, this moment provides a wonderful opportunity to further expose America's truths and address them. Black people are well-positioned for this moment if we choose to accept what is before us.

Consequently, despite slavery, empty promises by public and private sectors, and systemic racism, we have managed to keep our outlook and the promise of America alive. America is an experiment that needs nurturing. Black people, having built most of the infrastructure in this country, have a responsibility to build and maintain the notion of America as well. After all that has transpired in our history and after being treated as second-class citizens (or three fifths of a man, as a Black person is defined in the Constitution), one would think that there would be some honor, gratitude, or simple acknowledgment of all the labor we have exerted to make this country what it is.

Subsequently, the onus is still on us. This is the burden. As the sound of the Black Lives Matter movement took shape, the outcry began: "They buried us, but they didn't know we were seeds." The same sentiment can be said for the concept of the American dream. It is alive because we would not let it die.

These identification and relatability factors are the cornerstone of the Black leaders' superpower, particularly in an industry that is the perfect amalgamation of people, processes, and technology. This is the *benefit*. It rests on hope, diligence, perseverance, and all the other qualities you would think would be celebrated in any leader. However, heavy is the crown for many Black leaders in America and in health care, and one cannot wear that crown if his or her head is down.

Through this self-reflection period, I have learned that I like to let my actions speak much louder than my words. I subscribe to the following axiom, which I teach my students and mentors: "What is caught is more important than what is taught," meaning, "Watch what I do and not so much what I say." It has proven to be unorthodox and not celebrated much in health care, especially among a Black executive group that tends to be under the impression that

INTRODUCTION

there is only one way to achieve success in this industry and maybe in the country (the definition of assimilation).

Even in kindergarten, I tended to color outside the lines, as evidenced by positions that I have taken, partnerships that I have established, and investments that I have made. As stated, it has not been easy to go against the hospital administrator track, but I have been successful at maintaining who I am and how I can contribute. This project is my testament, and I want it to challenge and tests us all to change.

All of that has led to this. Actions speak louder than words only when those actions are pure and are making a difference and when the actors are weeded out to let true transformation occur. I do not think either are occurring in America, especially not within health care, so I felt compelled to share my thoughts.

Contrary to what you may think or the initial tone, this is my love letter to the country and to the healthcare industry. Americans and healthcare executives alike only want to hear what they want to hear. After hundreds of interviews and countless hours of research, I am ready to assume the mantle as the Black Jerry McGuire. If you saw the movie, Jerry wrote a "Mission statement" entitled

> **"Nobody knew health care could be so complicated."**
> **Donald Trump**
>
> **"And the same can be said for America."**
> **Gyasi C. Chisley**

"The Things We Think and Do Not Say." In most instances in America, scarcity increases the value of a commodity, but that supposition does not hold true for Black leaders. There is most certainly a scarcity of Black leadership in the country and particularly in health care. In fact, the scarcity is enforced and deliberate, which leads to assimilation and even invisibility.

Ralph Ellison wrote in *The Invisible Man*, "I was never more hated than when I was honest." So this love letter starts with the self-evident truths as the most contradictory figure in America, Thomas Jefferson, points out in the Declaration of Independence. However, I have never been more encouraged that the signs are there for this momentum to create an enduring movement that will lead to change. More importantly, I am ready to work with anyone who is inspired by this text to change our country and health care for good. It is *healthy* to be *disruptive*, and it is needed. It is time.

---

[1] "Eliminating the Black-White Wealth Gap Is a Generational Challenge," by Christian E. Weller and Lily Roberts, American Center for Progress (March 19, 2021).
[2] "Private Equity, Hedge Funds, and Investment Vehicles Industry in the US: Market Research Report," IBISWorld (July 26, 2021).
[3] "Waste in the US Health Care System: Estimated Costs and Potential for Savings," by William H. Shrank, Teresa L. Rogstad, and Natasha Parekh (JAMA Network, October 2019).
[3] PE Hub (2021).

Chapter 1

Working to Establish a Healthy Family in an Unhealthy Environment

"Pain is inevitable; suffering is optional." Unknown

In many cultures, the family unit serves as an anchor that gives people a sense of place, identity, and security. When the family functions in beneficial ways for each of its members, it creates an environment for them to thrive. Even across racial and socioeconomic strata, fully functional and supportive families can overcome great odds.

According to the International Federation for Family Development (IFFD), families are "basic and essential building blocks of societies," therefore their role is crucial in social development. "They bear the primary responsibility for the education and socialization of children as well as instilling values of citizenship and belonging in the society. Families provide material and non-material care and support to its members, from children to older persons or those suffering from illness, sheltering them from hardship to the maximum possible extent."[1]

Since it is in the home where such important development and protection should occur, the family and its environs should be at peak health. Unfortunately, that is often not the case for people of color. Lacking privilege and access, they are unable to secure many of life's basic necessities, much less excel and rise above their circumstances. They struggle with unemployment or underemployment; the lack of safe, affordable housing; food insecurities; socially determinative health problems; inadequate health care; mental health issues; and addictions. These stressors put an incredible strain on African American families, making them vulnerable to brokenness, dysfunction, and abuse.

The structure of this country has created perpetual and pervasive opportunities for the privileged to flourish, often at the expense of the disenfranchised, who are poor and usually reside in communities of color. The systems that have made this country thrive are rooted in racism and white supremacist positions and assertions. Slavery, capitalism, profit after catastrophe (wars and pandemics, for example) have not only prolonged the power struggle and issues of the downtrodden versus the privileged, but it has exacerbated over the years.

There is a difference of $164,000 between the average earnings of a white family compared to a Black family. According to *The Economist* magazine, the wealth gap has widened to the point that if a white family of four remained stagnant at the point it is in 2021, it would take a Black family of four nearly 200 years to equalize the earnings of a white family. This has purposefully destroyed communities of color and has created long-lasting fragmentation of the Black family. The intentional separation of the family unit dates back to slavery when slave owners knew that they would have more control if the family was disconnected and weakened.

CHAPTER ONE

Historically, African Americans have witnessed the breakup and destruction of their families from the moment they left the coasts of Africa and arrived in the Western Hemisphere as chattel. Slave masters did not honor the value of intact Black families because to do so would not put much profit on their ledgers. Even today, echoes of that trauma and injustice, Jim Crow laws, and racial discrimination still reverberate throughout Black families. This has not only negatively impacted socioeconomic opportunities for Black generational wealth, but has led to chronic and sustained health issues among Black people for centuries.

Thus, there is no question that Black people have not fared as well as our white counterparts physically, economically, or socially. Not only does Critical Race Theory exist, but it has been intensified over the years to ensure that the privileged remain privileged, while the Black family continues to struggle.

******

The health of Black families has been in peril since before we arrived on these shores. Our ancestors were packed tightly into large cargo ships and were trafficked to the colonies. Historians at Emory University say the trans-Atlantic slave trade was "the largest long-distance movement of people in history."[2]

The conditions aboard these ships were unsanitary and inhumane. To make the trips more profitable, approximately 600 Africans were forced into dark, cramped holding areas in the bottom of the ships. During the two-month harrowing journeys from Africa to the New World, or the Middle Passage, "men and women were physically separated . . . [and] packed together like cargo to sleep."[3] This environment left them susceptible to injury, disease, and death.

If they survived the trip to the Americas, Africans were sold to the highest bidders at slave markets. Slave owners were not

HEALTHY DISRUPTION

concerned about their slaves' emotional, mental, or social health; and they were concerned about their physical health only to the extent they needed the slaves to do the work for which they had been purchased.

On the vast plantations, slaves still wanted to form communities and families, but many of them were hesitant to do so. They soon learned slave owners were now making all the decisions for them, and they had little to no choice as to the direction their lives would take. Often, slave owners decided if and when slaves married and who would marry whom, and they separated families capriciously for profit or punishment.[4]

Slave children were warned from an early age that any day they could be sent alone to another plantation to work, or their families could be ripped apart at the whim of their owners. Generations of slaves were losing their tribal bonds and communities. In their tribes, a larger version of the family unit, they were protected and cared for with resources provided by the whole for the good of everyone.

Separated from community, slaves suffered emotionally and socially, as well as physically. Divided families meant they were no longer connected as they once had been, causing insecurities that were crippling. Often, they did not know what the next day would bring. Any day could be the last day a mother saw her children or a husband saw his wife.

In Africa, members of the tribe usually included those men and women who were known as "healers." They were in tune with the earth's rhythms and what it produced, which would be beneficial to soothe pains and heal diseases. Indigenous medicines were made from herbs and other materials found in nature, and the healing process was intricately tied to a tribe's religio-supernatural beliefs and their holistic approach to caring for the body while also

CHAPTER ONE

acknowledging mind and spirit. Imhotep was one of the first physicians on record, and he engendered a holistic approach to healing (not just medicine) in Africa. Today, many aspects of this approach have been lost in health care.

Separated from their healing heritage, slaves were forced to live in squalid housing, they were physically mistreated, and they were fed scraps or any food "not fit" for the slave owners' fine tables. The food given to slaves was rationed, and while some slaves ate better than others and they were allowed to eat fresh vegetables, many slaves subsisted on the toughest cuts of meat from pigs and cows, lard, molasses, and cornmeal. They supplemented their diet with whatever they could hunt for themselves, including wild animals (possums, raccoons, deer, turtle, squirrel, and rabbit), and they also foraged for nuts and berries.

In his two autobiographies—*The Story of My Life* and *Up From Slavery*—Booker T. Washington described his life on the Burroughs plantation in Virginia. He wrote that there were times when he could not eat breakfast because his mother was working the fields early in the morning. At those times, he would eat the boiled corn set aside to feed the cows and the pigs.[5]

So, the physical health of Black people has been under siege from the beginnings of slavery in the New World as they were treated as less than second-class citizens and had to learn how to survive on scraps. But according to Washington, in an ironic twist, there were food shortages due to blockades during the Civil War that affected plantation owners and their families more so than their slaves. "The owners had gotten used to eating expensive items prior to the war and the slaves were barely affected by lack of these items."[6] The slaves were able to go from chaos to creativity and preserve their families in wartime.

HEALTHY DISRUPTION

Even under these conditions, Black people showed resilience, which demonstrates our will to survive. However, the mental anguish of these conditions took its toll on Black families and communities. The anxiety and disquiet forcefully created by white supremacists was the cornerstone of breakdowns, despair, and disruption of many Black people—some in my own family. However, these issues were not often discussed, and Black people were left to internalize the wounds of the past.

America and the healthcare industry would do well to remember and return to that ancient wisdom and knowledge. Our ancestors called it *Sankofa*. This concept is derived from the Akan people of Ghana in West Africa. *Sankofa* is translated as "Go back and get it." One of the symbols used to depict *Sankofa* is "a mythical bird flying forward but with its head turned backward. The egg in its mouth represents the 'gems' or knowledge of the past upon which wisdom is based; it also signifies the generation to come that would benefit from that knowledge."[7] This was the basis for creating strong family units, community (tribal) ties, and a sense of belonging to previous generations. Conversely, it also fostered individual thinking and allowed for interpretation and input from the generations that would have to lead the tribe in the future.

I am often inspired by my mother's spirit of *Sankofa*. My mother, Joan Haddix Chisley, has already begun to lay the foundation for healthy families in our own extended family. In her book, *The Family Table, Too: Letters to My Granddaughter: Volume I*, she wrote, "I have explained continuously that the best way to pass on the cultural experiences, social value and communal mores of our previous generations—in other words, our African American History—is the retelling of their rich, colorful stories . . . [of] expectations,

CHAPTER ONE

responsibilities, and pride to disappointment and betrayal to losses and victories."[8]

Addressing the present, she encourages those who are soon to be our elders to begin writing their own stories to pass on. And with an eye to the future, she warns the generations to come to "ask more questions . . . and listen to the responses so [they] can expand on the vision [they] pass on to the next generation."[9] I wholeheartedly agree with my mother. I sincerely believe the spirit of *Sankofa* will benefit us and unite us as a people as we struggle to navigate the daily instances of racism, injustices, and disparities that unfortunately and deliberately persist today.

******

I grew up anxious.

Children are not mature enough to process complex emotional experiences. So when they see and live through more than they can handle, it produces stressors that affect their emotional, mental, and physical health. I lived through many of these stressors in my childhood that kept me in a perpetual state of fear, anxiety, worry, and rage. The residual effects of my childhood have left me with an ulcer, chronic diseases, and likely mental despair. I still struggle with resolving those issues to this day.

I am a Midwestern boy through and through. The integration of big city life with an appreciation for morals and values and wrapped in the possession of a ton of guilt and regrets is an appropriate description of a Black boy trying not only to survive but thrive in an unhealthy environment. The mere underpinning of these paradoxical themes creates anxiety.

I identify with and have a deep familiarity with the Northside of Milwaukee and the Southside of Chicago. Both are notoriously

HEALTHY DISRUPTION

high-crime, underserved, and impoverished areas. I know what it looks like to be afraid of being arrested, shot, and/or killed. (I have endured the first two and luckily escaped the third). I have also been falsely accused of crimes and beaten by the police. I had family members who did not have access to adequate housing, health care, and food. I saw up close and personal what happens when people did not know from one day to the next if they would have a paycheck and if that money would stretch far enough to pay for what they needed in order to survive. I witnessed family members fall into drug and alcohol addiction because they had no other outlet for their frustrations and failures when trying to provide for their families.

However, it was not the aspects of lack or death that scared me. I could process the act of going without and having to deal with loss. Although my parents worked hard and tried to instill a sense of community and foundation for me, I had classmates and family members who dealt with much more trauma and heartache. What terrified me the most was the instability of our situation. I do not think I have ever felt a fervent sense of security in my life. I have taken these anxieties with me to school, to college, to work, and to the boardroom. I know what these housing and food insecurities on any level can do to a home. Not unlike the uncertainties of slavery, families today can be ripped apart because of scarcity and lack when parents cannot adequately take care of themselves and their children.

*****

As an educator and a school psychologist, my mother was an agent for change and a disruptor of the system. For her family, she has been a beacon of light to her siblings and to new generations

CHAPTER ONE

as we have struggled with various forms of dysfunction over the years. Perhaps she was drawn into her career because she wanted to have an impact on the torment, horror, and day-to-day stressors that adversely influence impoverished children. She has had siblings who were diagnosed with mental disorders, so she is compassionate to those who are misunderstood and marginalized.

My mother's path to success was not easy, but her determination and resolve was forged in the hardship of the South and under the guidance of her family. My extended family has come so far yet has so far to go. It is hard for me to believe I am only three generations removed from slavery. My great-grandfather was a slave, but my maternal grandfather, Chalmus "Doc" Haddix, was a sharecropper who settled in Walnut, Mississippi, a little town about 70 miles south of Memphis.

> **"Count all the fingers and toes, I suppose you hope the little Black boy grows," Pete Rock & CL Smooth ("They Reminisce Over You")**

He had only a third-grade education but was one of the most insightful people I have ever known, although many of my family members would debate me on that statement. His truth rested on his relatability and his ability to couch his struggle into songs, stories, jokes, or musings.

My mom would pay me a few extra dollars to cut his hair toward the latter part of his life. It was during those times that he would showcase the power of brevity. He could encapsulate a whole lesson in a sentence or two. He had an indelible impact on me, probably for the same reasons he shaped my mother's perspectives, good and bad.

My granddaddy would extol stories of his childhood and accounts of his mistrials and misgivings with the privileged. He

HEALTHY DISRUPTION

would invoke signature phrases such as "Ya as wrong as two left shoes," "Ya as crooked as the letter S," for example. Through his cogitations, I found a pain and an outcry for things to be different. His reveries remind me of the song by Sam Cooke, "A Change Is Gonna Come." You could hear his soul, hope, and regret all in one narrative. I have attributed such sayings as "You can't let your reality check bounce" and "You can't be good and cheap at the same time" to my grandfather through his unique ability to tell a story. These are implicit qualities that I leverage today.

Health care as an industry, if not humanity itself, is all about relatability and sharing a certain pain, expressing empathy to another human being. I also find myself talking about my grandfather affectionately to colleagues and students and working hard to connect the life lessons he taught me into business lessons for others.

My grandfather was a sharecropper. Traditionally, sharecropping was an intricate but often uneven alliance between landowner and tenant. Both could benefit from the arrangement, but they also both assumed the risks that came with bad harvests or damaged land. Using his experience as a sharecropper, my grandfather taught my mother and her nine siblings many valuable lessons.

Two of those lessons are germane to the historic mindset of African American families. First, work hard. My grandfather's work ethic was unparalleled. He worked the fields with a vengeance, and he asked for more work so he could get as much out of the land as possible. He also worked extra jobs to provide for his large family, and he understood his solid work ethic would help him to do just that.

Second, absolutely nothing is promised, so whatever you have can be taken away at any time. My mother's family experienced this second principle when everything they had was taken away.

CHAPTER ONE

Doc crossed paths with the landowner, who was the local sheriff. He did not agree with what the sheriff was doing, and he did not mind speaking up about it. Of course, Doc always said, "Before you take a stand, you gotta know where you sit." After Doc spoke up, the sheriff kicked the Haddix family off his land; but I admire my grandfather for taking a stand, even though it cost him almost everything. Consequently, I see so much of him in my struggle today, which can be paired with the struggle of many Black men in this country.

My family left Mississippi and migrated north and then west in the early 1960s, first to Cleveland and Chicago and then to Milwaukee. African Americans who were part of the Great Migration in the twentieth century, moving from the agricultural South to the industrial North in search of better lives, must have been somewhat disappointed to find they did not necessarily leave racism and injustice behind in the sharecropping fields. Many Black families settled into these Northern communities and found themselves living and working shoulder to shoulder with other people who were living in poverty. Many would continue generations of struggle with poverty, food stamps and welfare benefits, substandard education and health care, inadequate housing, and crumbling families.

To cope, they internalized the stress of earning low wages and their lack of access to resources. These stressors took a toll on the health of many people who struggled to survive. It is extremely difficult to fathom neither current nor generational wealth when your health is compromised and basic care is only for the privileged. Make no mistake, health and wealth are inexorably tied.

In the early 1970s, my maternal grandmother died of a heart attack way too young at 60 years old. That same year, and not long after her death, one of her sons—my mother's brother—committed suicide. I firmly believe that the stressors of food insecurity, access to decent jobs and housing, and mental health concerns are just a few of the issues that my family has grappled with over the years. As a healthcare professional, it disturbs me that we are not able to provide better care for the most vulnerable in our communities and that those social determinants of health work against poor and minority families on every level.

*****

Slavery and discrimination and their related injustices and disparities have cast a long shadow over African American families. There have been stressors present in my family for generations. They are palpable in my own life and explain a great deal about how my family functions (or does not). My relatives are overly cautious and slow to open up to anyone outside our family unit. This is a trait we share with many disadvantaged and impoverished African American families.

The stressors for most families are generational, which is why their predicament seems inescapable. Children and youth experience difficulty overcoming the system because there are issues that trap them in poor neighborhoods, in underfunded public schools, and in dysfunctional families that are unable to support them. It is difficult to identify, root out, and resolve these stressors. Families become mired in pervasive despair, thinking there is no way out of poverty, out of the housing projects. They assume they will be poor for generations to come, and hopelessness sets in and hardens as the reality of the cyclical systemic nature of poverty becomes more clear.

My eyes were opened early through education to the dichotomy between white wealth and Black access. Purposefully, Black people do not have a lot of options nor resources. I learned that unless Black people were athletes, sold drugs, or were musically inclined, there was a high probability that they would not escape the systems that were set for them.

My mother promoted hope through education. I can recall examining together the philosophy behind the Talented Tenth, a concept endorsed by WEB DuBois, who wrote in an essay, "The Negro race, like all races, is going to be saved by its exceptional men,"[10] those "one in ten" college-educated black men who had risen through the ranks to become leaders in the community. DuBois was an eloquent scholar and, much like my mother, was enlightened by education. However, this belief flies in the face of everything that I have worked for and been able to achieve in my life.

I am where I am and who I am, and have been able to do what I have done, through the grace of opportunity that others have afforded me. I know I am not in the top tenth of any population—white, Black or otherwise—but I have been given a great gift of potential. Some people in positions of perceived power have created prospects for me to realize that potential.

This is the problem I have with the privileged. At times, they are so privileged that they do not recognize, let alone acknowledge, the fact they are where they are because someone cut a break for them, gave them something that they did not necessarily deserve, or gave them the benefit of a position that could materially change the trajectory for their families and their community.

Although unspoken and never fully acknowledged, the Civil Rights Movement—and more important, the Black Power promulgation—had a profound impact on my parents. The mentality of the group shaped them. From her study of the Black Panthers, my mother gleaned the principles of determination and self-sufficiency. She taught them to me so I would be able to take care of myself, prepare myself to challenge the disparities I would face, and provide a legacy for my own children.

HEALTHY DISRUPTION

I think it also led to my name. My first name means "wonderful and noble" in Swahili, and my middle name means "young warrior." How my mother named me signified that she wanted our nationality and ethnicity to be represented in my name. In addition, the name served as a promissory note of sorts from me to her on how I would work hard to represent our family.

Along with the hope she offered, my mother was intentional about having a plan for our family, which nurtured and protected us spiritually, emotionally, mentally, and physically. She excelled at making sure, no matter where we were or what our circumstances were, we made time for Kwanzaa and other important celebrations tethered to our culture, stayed together as much as possible, and shared what we had with one another. Her intentionality helped keep things in perspective and gave way to a platform for self-expression, much like our tribal instinct from our African ancestors.

Despite the tremendous pressure she was under as the go-to person in our family, the peacemaker who could bring different factions together, my mother never wavered. Her devotion to family still speaks to me today, and it is one of the reasons I am so unapologetic about calling out inequities and simultaneously open about sharing what I have with those I love.

******

I have been a healthcare executive for over 20 years. If I have learned anything, it is that everything is related to health, which makes us all in the business of health care. Unfortunately, society has not historically cared for those who are systemically and structurally disadvantaged, which includes many Black families like my own.

As my career matures, I find myself becoming more and more cynical. The deep divides that exist in the country are often cultivated within the healthcare industry (mandatory masks and vaccinations or caring for the uninsured, for example). When asked about being Black in America, writer James Baldwin said, "To be a Negro in this country and to be relatively conscious is to be in a rage all the time." I can relate. Because I am engaged in a country and an industry that embrace the concept of profit-over-people put into practice, and I know it is why many African Americans die too young; suffer for years with treatable, chronic illnesses and diseases; and lack resources to live healthier lives. The pandemic highlighted this inconceivable truth more than any event in recent memory.

I try to channel my anger and allow it to propel me into becoming an advocate for change for those who may not have a platform, the means to make their voices heard, or the access to express such disparity. However, if we are being honest, sometimes it seems nothing much has changed since our ancestors came through the Middle Passage in shackles and chains and were treated as less-than-human strictly for purposes of power, prestige, and profit for the privileged.

The physical dehumanization, oppression, and violence of slavery has morphed into present-day racism, neglect, police brutality, and denial of access to health care. Racism is pervasive and is structural, institutional, systemic, and individualized, particularly in the healthcare industry, where I see a myriad of disparities in the care families receive.

While the privileged enjoy better health care due to their inherent advantages and resources, often African Americans make do with inferior health care or forego seeking care altogether because of job instability; financial stressors; or inaccurate information around transformative, life-saving treatments, therapies, and medicines. Because of the disproportionate and intentional environs of African

HEALTHY DISRUPTION

Americans, social determinants of health are buttressed by an even greater need for comprehensive, customized, and holistic health care, especially preventative measures as it relates to certain disease types because conditions are poor.

According to the Centers for Disease Control and Prevention (CDC), *social determinants of health* (SDOH) are "conditions in the places where people live, learn, work, and play that affect a wide range of health and quality-of life-risks and outcomes."[11] The World Health Organization says, "These circumstances are shaped by the distribution of money, power, and resources at global, national, and local levels. They state social determinants of health are mostly responsible for health inequities—the unfair and avoidable differences in health status seen within and between countries."[12]

When families wrestle with adverse conditions in spaces that should be safe and healthy, they experience stressors that negatively affect their physical and mental health. The Centers for Medicaid and Medicare Services (CMS) have also identified social determinants of health as fundamental indicators in establishing a person's quality of life. I contend that people's zip codes goes much further in determining their health outcomes than their genetic code. The American healthcare system, mired in politics and profit and based on a racist premise, has traditionally failed at acknowledging, recognizing, and addressing community health as a solution to some of the health crises we currently face.

In spite of the healthcare industry's slow acceptance of essential concepts for transformation and incremental approach to change, there have been significant strides throughout history. Taking a wide-lens angle on American history, progress in health care, albeit incremental, was made during three presidential administrations.

CHAPTER ONE

While dealing with the Great Depression and conceptualizing the New Deal, President Franklin Roosevelt also signed into law the Social Security Act of 1935, giving way to the creation of Medicare some 30 year later. The Social Security Act recognized that seniors ages 65 and older should be eligible for certain benefits (retirement, stipends, and health care). Many countries had already established similar programs, but the United States inferred that this was a groundbreaking, innovative benefit and it was the sole country taking care of its senior citizens.

It was not until 1965 that President Lyndon Johnson signed amendments to the Social Security Act forming Medicare, a government-issued insurance program for seniors, and Medicare, an insurance program for those under a certain threshold that the government determines (and changes) known as "the federal poverty line." Unfortunately, as imagined and predicted, Medicare benefits went to the most privileged first and did not start trickling down to many Black beneficiaries until 1966. Similarly, Black people had to overcome many administrative hurdles to prove they were poor enough to receive Medicaid.

During that same year, President Johnson also signed the Voting Rights Act of 1965. This landmark legislation eradicated many of the barriers to the basic right to vote that Black people had faced since Reconstruction. Dr. Martin Luther King Jr., John Lewis, and others were instrumental in pressuring Johnson to sign the bill. Sadly, this act is still under attack today in Georgia and other states.

Under President Barack Obama's administration, the Affordable Care Act (ACA) was signed in March 2010. The ACA decreased the number of uninsured in this country, a number that teetered at approximately 48-50 million during its first 18 months of inception.

HEALTHY DISRUPTION

Although the rollout was botched and the argument for support could have been stronger, the ACA achieved a great feat and insured many of the disenfranchised in this country by expanding Medicaid, among other tactics. For the first time in modern history, there was a government-established healthcare program, using private exchanges that allowed Americans to choose their own insurance products without an employer-based option.

******

Slavery, racism, and injustice have cast a long, dark shadow over the Black family and its pursuit of equality. Personally, I have witnessed how it reached beyond my great-grandfather's enslavement, my grandfather's sharecropping, my mother's teaching, and my administering. My family's story is not unlike the story of many Black families. In fact, my family's story is an American story. It is a story that is sad, at times progressive, and fraught with inconsistencies that create cynicism, mental instability, physical afflictions, and financial strife.

Within the failed construct of this country and the healthcare industry, I want to do for it much like what my mother did for me. I want to establish hope, alternatives, and change. I am working to share with the industry the spirit of *Sankofa* and allow those who identify with the sentiment a platform for transformation, a growth mindset of determination, and self-reliance—concepts the Black community has incorporated during our strides for equity in this country.

Establishing a healthy Black family is possible, even in the clutch of horrific racist conditions that this country created and continues to systemically sustain. The African American's ancestry was built on the premise of community health and holistic cures and

CHAPTER ONE

medicines. The American healthcare system is slowly embracing this concept.

A country and an industry is only as good as its most disenfranchised citizen. This country, as well as its healthcare system, must leverage our opportunities and work together to disrupt not only chronic diseases, but chronic paradigms that perpetuate poverty, dependence, and pain and inhibit progress, proliferation of innovation, and profit. Creating this perspective, I, like my grandfather, had to understand first where I sit so that I am able to take a stand. I am praying that others will join this critical campaign and effort.

---

[1] "The Crucial Role of Families," International Federation for Family Development in General Consultative Status With the United Nation's Economic and Social Council, 2017 (un.org/ecosoc/sites/www.un.org.ecosoc/files/files/en/integration/2017/IFFD.pdf).

[2] "Documenting Slave Voyages," Kimber Williams, Emory University, June 2019 (https://news.emory.edu/features/2019/06/slave-voyages/index.html).

[3] "Documenting Slave Voyages."

[4] "Enslaved Couples Faced Wrenching Separations, or Even Choosing Family Over Freedom," Tera W. Hunter, History.com, September 20, 2019 (https://www.history.com/news/african-american-slavery-marriage-family-separation).

[5] "A 19th-Century Slave Diet," Booker T. Washington National Monument, National Park Service, Department of the Interior (https://www.nps.gov/bowa/learn/historyculture/upload/the-final-slave-diet-site-bulletin.pdf).

[6] "A 19th-Century Slave Diet."

[7] "*Sankofa*," University of Rochester (https://www.rochester.edu/diversity/faculty-staff/resource-groups/sankofa/).

[8] *The Family Table, Too: Letters to My Granddaughter: Volume I*, Joan Haddix Chisley (Outskirts Press, 2020); Kindle edition.

[9] *The Family Table, Too: Letters to My Granddaughter: Volume I*.

[10] *The Negro Problem*, Booker T. Washington (1903).

[11] "Social Determinants of Health: Know What Affects Health," Centers for Disease Control and Prevention (May 6, 2021)

[12] "What Are Social Determinants of Health?" CDC (March 10, 2021).

[13] "Racism, Inequality, and Health Care for African Americans," Jamila Taylor, The Century Foundation, September 2019 (https://tcf.org/content/report/racism-inequality-health-care-african-americans/).

Chapter 2

Building Healthy Communities for Real Equity

"Freedom is a road seldom traveled by the multitude." Fredrick Douglas

There is a stark distinction between health equity and health equality. Many people, even African Americans, confuse these important concepts. Because capitalism is the primary principle of this country, it is important that ownership and control be the predominate precursor to the work that is needed to gain equality. Equity is synonymous with the language of "owning land" at the turn of the twentieth century; and land is power, even now. *Equity* is ownership, stake, control, and governance of a particular entity. *Equality* occurs when two people are treated the same and have the same opportunities to gain equity. Achieving equity should be the goal, first and foremost, and equality is a vision I may not see in my lifetime.

HEALTHY DISRUPTION

In spite of all the positions that I have held and the accomplishments I have achieved within the healthcare industry, I have yet to be treated as an equal executive, particularly at the onset of any role. Whereas a white professional with less experience is usually welcomed without reservation, evaluation, speculation, or equivocation. Subsequently, I have to explain my background, why I am qualified, and why I should continue to be considered just to glean additional responsibility. Moreover, I know that those same privileged people who are in power and can distribute authority are tearing me down and working to destroy my character in the background.

This character and professional destruction serves two purposes: One, it gives the appearance of a Black man assuming a role that he is unqualified for and diminishes his experience so that he does not ascend too quickly through the ranks. Two, it gives more credence and credibility to the white counterpart. In a capitalistic society (versus *Ubuntu*), there always has to be a good person and a bad person and never simply a person just working together to address issues.

Equity mitigates this power struggle. Instead of slicing the pie and working to maintain your specific slice, equity gives inroads to growing the pie or owning the pie for yourself. With equity, the pathway to power is put back in the hands of the oppressed. It is the growth mindset, and it is what is needed to, at the very least, have a shot at equality in the future.

My daughter is in middle school and has already been called a nigger twice to her face (and likely countless other times behind her back). It hurt. It could be easily dismissed by saying it is just the school that is racist or that it is the region that is racist. I would contend that America is racist and the capitalistic mentality certainly has racist undertones. Therefore, I cannot change racist kids calling

CHAPTER TWO

my daughter names, but what I can do is ensure that she inherits our real estate interests in seven states and my stake in over 20 business entities. It is not necessarily equality, but it definitely lends itself to equity.

Our communal sensibilities have once again been ripped away from us. What has happened within black communities has been unhealthy in the extreme and has made us vulnerable. There are so many perils around housing, food, safety, and access to all things health-related, which has made our communities fragmented.

African Americans' pursuit of equity must be channeled and strategized in the appropriate manner. Black people have never controlled their own communities. If there is an instance where Black people are getting close to ownership, it is usually stolen through a policy or a law, gentrified, or burned. Historically, promises have been bestowed on Black people by the government, but those promises were not kept. For example, 40 acres and a mule were promised to newly freed slaves after the Civil War, but that promise never came to fruition. Also, communities such as Greenwood in Tulsa, Oklahoma, were developed so Black people could enjoy ownership. However, many of those same communities were destroyed by white supremacists.

Knowing there is power in that type of control, the undercutting continues to plague communities of color. It is systematically used as a weapon for oppression. It is essential that Black leaders work to reinvest in disenfranchised communities. If equity is somewhat of a safe harbor to realizing the American dream, Black people must be safe in our own communities; but that only happens when we control the lion's share of businesses and operations. Equity is the clearest and most expedient path to that type of control.

HEALTHY DISRUPTION

*****

For Black people, slavery was our crucible. Through it, Black people were acquainted with being snatched from our homeland, held in bondage, beaten, torn from our families, living with deprivation, and being treated as chattel. Even today, we live with the residue of that inhumane and cruel treatment. Consequently, we also learned how to survive and even thrive at times.

During the last two years of the American Civil War, the nation entered the era of Reconstruction, which lasted from 1863 to 1877. During Reconstruction, "the U.S. government undertook the task of integrating nearly four million formerly enslaved people into society after the Civil War bitterly divided the country over the issue of slavery."[1]

For newly freed slaves, this was a brief but golden age of progress and change. African Americans began to return to many of the communal concepts their ancestors had left behind before crossing the Middle Passage. The diaspora came together and established their communities so that they could once again live with one another. They used the knowledge they had gleaned as slaves to tend and harvest the land.

The country was still severely divided, but as a collective segment, African Americans began to heal. For the first time, Black leadership was ascending in politics, which gave them more power and authority to affect change for the lives of those who formerly had been so dependent on the whims of the privileged. Blacks were able to participate in the democratic process and leverage their freedom to fully exercise their rights as citizens. "Rather than passive victims of the actions of others, African Americans were active agents in shaping Reconstruction."[2] And because their families were not being ripped apart by slave masters, their family structure was strengthened, which was beneficial to their mental, emotional, and financial stability.

This period of social change soon came to an end, and the nation was plunged back into a dark period of segregation and injustice for African Americans. As the efforts gained during Reconstruction were gradually rolled back, oppressive practices and policies, such as Jim Crow, were eventually made law. Once again, the health and welfare of Black people in this country were in peril.

Two major institutions were forged in that crucible and emerged from slavery, Reconstruction, and the Jim Crow era: the Black church and Historically Black Colleges and Universities (HBCUs). During slavery, the Black church gave hope to the enslaved, many of whom could not even read the Bible from which it established its doctrine. However, it gave them a basis for community apart from the master and the backbreaking work they had to do from sunup to sundown.

Though most of them could not read from the Bible or a hymnal, they listened to sermons about heaven and freedom from their toils and worry as they sang "Nobody Knows the Trouble I've Seen," "Swing Low, Sweet Chariot," and "Go Down, Moses." Frederick Douglass wrote, "They were tones, loud, long and deep, breathing the prayer and complaint of souls boiling over with the bitterest anguish. Every tone was a testimony against slavery, and a prayer to God for deliverance from chains. . . . Those songs still follow me, to deepen my hatred of slavery, and quicken my sympathies for my brethren in bonds."[2]

The church grounded Black people "in bonds," and gave them a unified voice as they preached and sang about freedom. Black people

HEALTHY DISRUPTION

were robbed of their native languages of Akan, Igbo, and Yoruba, among others. Through the gospel of the Black church and hymnals, they could talk about themes that represented their hope for justice. Slavery was responsible for the division and brokenness among Black people, but the church provided a platform free from the master's oppression (at least for a few hours) and reignited a sense of community.

The unfortunate truth is that white supremacists realized early on that the Black church served as a staple, an energy source, for the Black community. The Ku Klux Klan and other white terrorists bombed Black churches, barged into services to intimidate parishioners, and fired shots into their sanctuaries. Some of these instances were reported and publicized, but many were not. Despite the 1964 Birmingham bombing, which killed four girls, to the 2016 mass shooting in a South Carolina church, where nine people were shot, Black people have worked to keep the church a safe haven for the community.

Like most innovation within the Black community, HBCUs came by way of hardship. The nineteenth century birthed opportunities for higher education for Blacks. Throughout slavery, education for slaves was forbidden. They could be beaten or killed for learning how to read or write. In 1837, a Quaker named Richard Humphreys founded the first HBCU, Cheyney University, in Pennsylvania. There are now over 100 HBCUs, and each has its own story and unique trajectory. The common thread interwoven through them all is how they served African Americans who had been excluded from mainstream educational spaces.

Because of the foresight of many Black people to become educated and the philanthropy of some to fund HBCUs, Reconstruction

CHAPTER TWO

spurred growth in Black entrepreneurship. During slavery, Black people were mostly dependent on masters and white-owned businesses to provide essential goods and services. However, after the Civil War, they were placed in the position of having to establish their own businesses because white business owners would invoke Jim Crow policies and not serve freed Black people. Blacks had to build their own communities with Black dentists, doctors, shop owners, banks, and schools.

Black people discovered that there was power in proximity. The doctor lived next door to the mill worker, who lived next to the schoolteacher and the grocer. At the height of segregation, communities thrived because they were strongly interconnected. An example of a thriving community was that of Greenwood in Tulsa, also known as "the Black Wall Street." Black people were investing in the community because they were not allowed to "cross the tracks" into the southern side of the city.

This community was made up of Black professionals, entertainers, business owners, and educators. However, Greenwood was destroyed when a white woman falsely accused a Black man of sexual assault and jealous white residents of Tulsa burned down the entire neighborhood. After attempts to reestablish Greenwood as a neighborhood, today it still struggles to remain viable due to gentrification laws, lack of resources, and little financial support.

It was during this time, however, that Black people established their own hospitals. The first black-owned and black-operated hospital was Providence Hospital in Chicago. It was founded by Dr. Daniel Hale Williams in 1891 and provided training for nurses and interns.[3] Like most services offered during this period, segregation required separate services for Black people and white people, which meant a difference between how Black people and white people accessed health care. Within this construct, Providence was severely under-resourced and labeled as the Black hospital with poor outcomes. In the nineteenth century, this laid the groundwork for the pervasive thinking that Black people were second-class citizens, no better than they were during slavery.

Today, hospitals on the Southside of Chicago still grapple with the stigma of being in a predominately Black area. This judgment and treatment subjected the already vulnerable Black communities to predatory healthcare studies and practices. For nearly 50 years, Black women were the target of racial eugenics modeled after Nazi programs during the Holocaust. From the 1920s to the 1970s, Black women were subjected to forced sterilizations, often without their knowledge.[4]

One of the most egregious instances in living memory happened in Macon County, Alabama. Blacks were treated as lab rats during the Tuskegee Experiment. This study, begun in 1932, was officially known as the Tuskegee Study of Untreated Syphilis in the Negro Male. It included 600 men, most of whom were "poor and illiterate sharecroppers." Though there was no treatment for syphilis when the study began, in 1947, researchers found that penicillin was an effective treatment. However, the medication was withheld from participants in the Tuskegee study. It was not until 1972 that the public was made aware of the atrocities that had taken place and the study ended.[5]

*****

Having experienced social and economic injustices since arriving on American shores, Black people have become less trusting and jaded because of the persistent mistreatment, prejudices, and policies

CHAPTER TWO

that have derided us for generations. It is not surprising that when politicians or corporations seem to take an interest in Black communities, there is a healthy level of skepticism and the suspicion that there is an ulterior motive.

Flint, Michigan, is a city that is nearly 60 percent Black, with over 39 percent living below the federal poverty line. As early as 2014, residents in Flint in predominately Black neighborhoods complained about the appearance and taste of the city's water. It was not until 2019 that the matter was investigated and acknowledged. Government and city officials indicated that the water was contaminated with lead and possibly other harmful bacteria but insisted that the water was clean and suitable to drink. However, researchers showed that the adverse health effects residents complained of could be linked to the water.

The contaminated water was discovered to come from faulty pipes from a water supply that funneled to primarily low-income areas. However, this fact was discovered decades earlier, but nothing was done to clean up the water supply. I believe that if this were a predominately white city in a different income bracket, there would have been an outcry and far more urgency to address the problem. This is a recent example of how the oppressed and disenfranchised are treated in this country, but there have been countless other instances. This is another example of why Black people mistrust the government and those in perceived power.

It is difficult to build and to establish healthy communities when people do not trust those who have the resources to offer their help and support. Moreover, incidents such as the Flint water crisis have been intentionally ignored to keep valuable resources from those citizens who need it most. America's continued marginalization

HEALTHY DISRUPTION

and its failure to act and advocate for its disenfranchised citizens also prevents citizens from acquiring the most basic needs, such as affordable housing, sound education, and quality health care.

*****

Charles Dickens wrote of London, "It was a tale of two cities." In Chicago, it is a tale of one city with two identities.

This have never been made more clear than in my adopted hometown of Chicago. Today, the differences between the North Side and the South Side could not be more stark. Although these two neighborhoods are separated by roughly a four- to five-mile-radius—essentially 50 blocks—there is a huge disparity between them. Compared to North Side neighborhoods, the South Side has a life expectancy of more than 30 years shorter. Currently, this is the largest life expectancy gap in the United States. Needless to say, South Side zip codes are primarily Black, brown, and poor, while the North Side neighborhoods boast some of the wealthiest incomes per capita.

Per every square mile, the North Side has a healthcare facility, clinic, or hospital nearly all the way to the northern suburbs. However, the South Side has a high rate of hospital closures. About 40 percent of South Side hospitals have closed in the last decade. These are factors that protect more privileged communities and exacerbate the suffering of others, purely based on their zip codes.

These disparities are universal in almost every metropolis in America and have led to disturbing and widening division between Black and white wealth. Black families have only a fraction of the wealth of white families, leaving them more economically insecure and fewer opportunities for economic mobility. This insecurity then exposes a host of social determinants of health that make people of color more susceptible to diseases that worsen when access to care is an issue. According to the Center for American Progress,[6]

- The wealth gap currently stands at an average of $188,000 for white households compared to a startling $24,000 average for Black families (2021).
- Black people in the workforce are 50 percent less likely to graduate from college compared to white counterparts.
- Roughly 45 percent of Black families own their own homes compared to 75 percent of whites who are homeowners in this country.
- Of all the Black households, approximately 72 percent live below the federal poverty line compared to under 31 percent for white households.
- Black men are eight times more likely than white men to be incarcerated.
- Black men are 20 times more likely to be arrested as compared to white men.
- Black households have far less access to tax-advantaged forms of savings, due in part to a long history of employment discrimination and other discriminatory practices.
- A well-documented history of mortgage market discrimination means that black people are significantly less likely to be homeowners than whites, which means they have less access to the savings and tax benefits that come with owning a home.
- Persistent labor market discrimination and segregation also force black Americans into fewer and less advantageous employment opportunities, meaning they also have

HEALTHY DISRUPTION

> "I'm from the murder capital where they murder for capital."
>
> **Kanye West**

less access to stable jobs, good wages, and retirement benefits.

Of all the social determinants of health, employment is chief among them. Nearly 80 percent of Americans access their health insurance through their employers. However, unemployment is disproportionately high in communities of color. This was especially heightened during the pandemic. In addition, Black people often possess higher risk factors associated with service industry jobs, which may not offer health insurance. This system has been in place for too long and excludes many of the lower-middle class, working poor, and unemployed.

Leveraging my years of experience within the healthcare industry and drawing from communal concepts that my mother instilled in me from Kwanzaa observance, I am working inside and outside the industry to address these grave disparities. One important lesson in this plight is that the privileged definitely value where they live. They work to ensure the value of their homes and that their investments are protected at all costs. There have been clauses in FHA loans and through the HUD program that stipulate who can qualify for loans and live in certain neighborhoods. This has adversely affected Black people from moving into more progressive neighborhoods and obtaining home loans.

I have seen the privileged think broader, invest in other ventures, engage with big ideas, and take risks because usually the investment and value of their homes are protected. They can leverage more and risk more, borrow against their homes, and sell them if necessary, a benefit purposefully elusive to many Black people in this country.

CHAPTER TWO

It was not until I had an opportunity to live in a designated white neighborhood that I realized this truth.

Given these epiphanies, I began to reflect on my upbringing and felt spiteful because there was no one in my circle to impart any wisdom about investments, home ownership, and entrepreneurship. I thought about all the atrocities and ills that emanate from these intentional disparities. Taking the *Rich Dad, Poor Dad* lessons to heart, it was clear that I had to work harder to evangelize to all who would listen about the importance of investments, real estate, and the need to start early with sound financial habits.

These experiences confirmed for me that one of the reasons Black communities cannot heal is because of structural systems that have been levied against us. However, Black families, investors, and philanthropists have an opportunity here as well. Much like the mindset of the previous generations when segregation was at its height, Black people took matters into our own hands by building businesses, creating avenues for others to learn and to educate themselves, establishing banks and loan programs, and promoting healthier options where food insecurities exist.

Once Black people recalibrate themselves with the growth mindset of our ancestors and the spirit of *Sankofa*, we will realize healthier families, thriving neighborhoods, quality education, and easier access to care. If Black people can realign our families to let generational wealth be the goal and delay gratification on items that depreciate in value (cars, clothes, and jewelry, for example), we will begin to actively pursue what was promised to us shortly after Reconstruction: our 40 acres and a mule.

Equality is the vision, but it only comes through equity as the tactic. Equity engenders a certain power and freedom because one

HEALTHY DISRUPTION

can leverage it. This is the quickest path to some semblance of equality, even in a racist society like America.

*****

A person's zip code is a far more apt indicator of one's health versus their genetic code. This disproportionately affects people of color. This is a component of the "black tax" that people of color pay. Where a person lives could determine their success, happiness, and overall life expectancy. I find it appalling that in one of the wealthiest countries in the world these disparities are so readily apparent. Then again, American was founded on these faulty practices and consistently profits from them.

Many people are trapped in crumbling neighborhoods that have substandard housing, failing public schools, food deserts, high rates of unemployment and crime, and no access to quality health care. It is not as simple as telling the people in these zip codes to do better. They need the resources to improve their communities, or they need a pathway out. Neither answer is easy. As late-night TV host Trevor Noah wrote, "We tell people to follow their dreams, but you can only dream of what you can imagine, and, depending on where you come from, your imagination can be quite limited."[7]

Though partnering with government, public, and private entities will increase the number of resources and support we can inject into marginalized communities, I do not recommend waiting for them to rush in and make everything better. I trust the people who actually live in these communities to know what they need most, and we should hear their voices first. I want to encourage them to begin the work of building and rebuilding their communities, but I also want to help them have the most effective tools, knowledge, and resources to accomplish that end. Promoting the infusion of capital, attaining

CHAPTER TWO

equity, building private business with venture and angel investors, and working to eradicate crooked policies that force Black people out of their own neighborhoods once they are improved should all be top of mind.

Jason Reynolds and Ibram X. Kendi, authors of *Stamped: Racism, Antiracism, and You*, wrote, "We can't attack a thing we don't know. That's dangerous. And . . . foolish. It would be like trying to chop down a tree from the top of it. If we understand how the tree works, how the trunk and roots are where the power lies, and how gravity is on our side, we can attack it, each of us with small axes, and change the face of the forest."[8]

Legislation is a powerful tool to create the opportunities needed to "change the face of the forest." But it should not be the only weapon in the arsenal. Politics is a fickle and dirty game that often leverages disenfranchised people every election cycle to get in or stay in power. "Politics is brutal. . . . [and] at its best [it is] an imperfect means to an altruistic end."[9]

We ought to start asking ourselves the distinctive and uncommon questions: Are we using the best talent available? Are we partnering with the right entities in vulnerable communities? Are we actively helping to removing the roadblocks to healthy lives? How can we better connect with diversified thought leaders and different groups of people?

One of the paths to more diversity in the industry is to look more closely at HBCUs. HBCUs can be a source of more of the talent that corporate America needs, including the healthcare space. The men and women who graduate from these schools can provide the representation in communities of color that usually do not see health care providers who look like them. HBCU graduates can provide a link to the people in zip codes who are the hardest to reach.

Education and health, like most of the social determinants, are inextricably tied. Therein lies the importance and power of HBCUs. African Americans who graduate from these schools provide the industry a wider array of the care delivery methodologies for and by Black people. It is obvious that we need more people who look like us and who can bridge those racial and class divides to foster trust in giving care in underserved and underprivileged communities.

Initially, I did not plan to attend an HBCU. I was totally sold on my limited ability to play basketball and thought that would provide a route to the next level. From there, I would work to be scouted by some NBA executive. After taking the SATs during my senior year, I scored reasonably well and was accepted to Princeton. For the first time, I was at a crossroads and had to make a decision for me, for my family, and for the culture. Naturally, I consulted my mentor, Dr. William Finlayson, a graduate of Morehouse, as well as a pillar in the Black community in Milwaukee.

Dr. Finlayson graduated in the same class as the Reverend Dr. Martin Luther King Jr. in 1948. Dr Finlayson saw qualities in me that I did not see in myself, and he has helped me achieve my greatest accomplishments. He helped me see that sometimes the answers are so obvious if we are attentive and realize there are no coincidences. I am confident Dr. Finlayson, among other key people, was put in my life to steer me to Morehouse. Many great things have happened to me and influenced major life decisions because I was a student, and now an alumnus, of Morehouse College.

Although I was not quite sure that I fit the stereotypical "Morehouse Man" and did not possess the pedigree or mystique that most

CHAPTER TWO

17- or 18-year-olds held, my experience at Morehouse awakened my soul. It challenged me to explore things outside my own life experiences. Morehouse encouraged me to think critically and to resist conformity, and it propelled me to my purpose today.

Morehouse gave me the tools to become an effective leader, and my greatest weapon has been teaching. I learned that to teach is to transform. I recognize the potential in the next generation, and I am willing to shepherd them through the ranks to make room for new, innovative leadership. Because what is needed in the industry are more leaders who have courage, empathy, compassion, and a self-awareness of something greater than themselves. We need a system that will welcome them, listen to them, challenge them, and trust them. Currently, the industry intimidates leaders and potential leaders, who are often afraid to speak out.

There is no question that HBCUs, like Morehouse, are producing the leaders of today and the next generation of trailblazers, including Vice President Kamala Harris. There is a healthy pipeline that is germinating throughout the country from HBCUs. However, HBCUs need support by way of the following:

- **Secure their future.** Many HBCUs do not have endowments like major state and public institutions.
- **Deepen their fields of study.** Expanded curricula will help encourage broader worldviews and skills. With more fields of study also comes the opportunity to attract a whole new base of students and professors on the tenure track.
- **Strengthen their ties to the community.** There is an opportunity to use those investments to fuel economic activity in the neighborhoods and cities where these

HEALTHY DISRUPTION

HBCUs are located and where those students and professors live and work.
- **Go beyond the capital and endowment.** HBCUs can benefit from expertise and various networks to open doors to new possibilities and investing time into the institution and its future graduates.
- **Partnerships.** HBCUs have benefited through engaging with corporations, foundations, and the federal government. They have also partnered with traditional universities to develop curricula and degree programs.

Currently, Black people comprise about 20 percent of the service jobs within the healthcare industry, but only about three percent of the leadership and care delivery jobs, which are far more prestigious and pay higher wages. For an industry that accounts for about 20 percent of the nation's economy and $4 trillion in spending each year, there is a dearth of Black professionals, administrators, and leaders within the healthcare industry. This is most noticeable when providers are caring for African Americans who account for most of the patient population within hospitals, particularly in urban settings. Large employers and the private sector can play a significant role in establishing stronger communities as well.

The following are areas where companies can make a major impact in people's lives with more mindful approach to funding, specifically in communities of color:

- **Employment.** Hire community residents, build focus groups on what matters most to the community, and establish social impact funds to help other small businesses thrive.

- **Food.** Regardless of the products and services, establish farmers markets, and offer discounts to local grocery stores for employees.
- **Housing.** Partner with the government and other public entities to establish programs that will facilitate home ownership for employees.
- **Education.** Incorporate tuition vouchers and loan forgiveness programs for employees; offer scholarships to top employees; when recruiting, place new recruits in the most underserved areas, and offer them incentives.
- **Health care.** Offer free screenings for employees, decrease premiums for those who practice healthy behavior, give extra pay for vaccinations and regular check-ups, give access to digital services, and steer employees to the ACA exchanges for greater choice.

These actions would not be difficult for most mid-cap to large companies. They can leverage their size to influence the policies that would help make these kinds of partnerships possible.

Rather than recreate the wheel, we can also use the tools that are already at our disposal. The ACA mandates that nonprofit hospitals demonstrate community benefit and conduct Community Health Needs Assessments, which can be a useful map in helping us identity where we need action in the community. Using these data, we can review and monitor key performance indicators (KPI) for most communities since health is interconnected to other social aspects of any community. Poor health is a symptom of a much bigger problem within our society and is a justice issue. We can directly connect life expectancy to income inequality.

HEALTHY DISRUPTION

According to the Economic Policy Institute, income inequality has risen in every state since the 1970s.[10] The Health Inequality Project measures differences in life expectancy by income.[11] Their research, published in the *Journal of the American Medical Association*,[12] shows that the richest American men live 15 years longer than the poorest men, while the richest American women live ten years longer than the poorest women.

In addition, lower-income families have more stressful lives,[13] according to the American Psychological Association (APA). Stressors related to social and economic disadvantage have demonstrable downstream effects on a wide range of psychological, neurobiological, physiological, and behavioral processes related to health.[14] We cannot change these truths until we confront these truths.

In order to build healthy communities, I challenge our most disenfranchised and marginalized communities and their supporters to consider the following:

1. **Speak up and out, early and often.** Advocates, influencers, and leaders need to fight for specific needs in specific zip codes and communities, such as food, safety, health, and education. They need to work together to connect the dots among these interconnected issues. Healthy confrontation is needed to bring awareness. Get "upstream" before issues become dire, and influence policymakers to take action. We need to be willing to disrupt and dismantle the platforms that keep our communities from growing and improving.

2. **Build coalitions to create change.** Seek out minority-owned businesses, and patronize and help fund them. Partner with them (create a formal partnership with nondisclosure

agreements, contractual obligations, and milestones) within your respective field. These collaborations can bring credibility to small businesses, while other casual partnerships can aid burgeoning businesses (donating t-shirts, volunteering on the weekends, and offering assistance with marketing and social media). Black communities can and will flourish if the silos are broken.

3. **Connect your networks.** Take the coalitions that have been built, existing and new, and expand their influence. Opportunities abound not only for networking, but in using social media for good to galvanize the masses and bringing together people, groups, and organization that may not seem to fit naturally but have a growth mindset and a concern for the communities in which they serve.

I also recommend that those who choose to help build and rebuild communities do so mindfully and through a lens of support, not with superiority, condemnation, or pity. The disenfranchised communities have reached their current state through purposeful oppression and structural racist platforms pitted against them. Most communities are willing to partner to make their communities healthier and better. The voiceless have voices. Unfortunately, they have been ignored for far too long. When we empower communities to be healthier, it ultimately improves all communities.

Early in my career, I was fortunate to work for a Federally Qualified Health Center (FQHC), and I currently serve on the board for a regional FQHC outfit. FQHCs were established by the government, and funding was expanded under the ACA in 2010. They provide access to primary care in many impoverished communities.

HEALTHY DISRUPTION

They offer a basic pharmacy or a means of getting prescriptions filled, which lessens the number of people who go the more expensive route of using the emergency room to get prescriptions. Some FQHCs offer dental services; diagnostics, such as basic lab and imaging services; and some mental health resources.

However, I have been disappointed in the lack of support that these centers receive. FQHCs are probably the most dependent agency on the government that I have ever seen. If funding is late, missed, mismanaged, or cut from the municipal budget, FQHCs have to furlough employees for a week or more and try to reopen when funding is returned. This inconsistency leads to further lack of support and missed opportunities to care for patients and become a healthcare staple for the community.

I believe the days of care delivery within clunky brick-and-mortar buildings should be laid to rest. The pandemic accelerated two important concepts in health care: telehealth and home health care. The industry has flirted with these concepts for decades; but because of the given quarantine protocols, the healthcare industry was forced to reevaluate and incorporate these valuable tools not just for communication and interaction with patients, but for actual care.

Home health care is likely the product of the past when doctors still made house calls. From anecdotal evidence, I have learned that not as many doctors performed house calls in Black communities as they did in white communities. However, as the industry becomes more clinically savvy and less regulated, home health operations have grown. Home health care is an excellent method not only for care delivery in a space where the patient feels comfortable and can coalesce on his or her terms, but it also gives providers keen insight into some of the social determinants of health that may be impacting that particular patient (food, resources, and environment, for example).

Telehealth was highly regulated from a state and federal level. Those regulations were relaxed somewhat during the pandemic, and I hope they will continue to ameliorate as we continue to see the value in telehealth. The ability to connect with a healthcare professional via electronic device is convenient and will likely improve health outcomes.

Despite resistance to promoting these healthcare resources, Black communities have benefited from this technology that was available but nascent for years. Home health care and telehealth alone could change the antiquated and unsafe environment of health care, particularly for disenfranchised communities. These avenues of care could transform the current healthcare space—the stale hospital or doctor's office approach—to an infrastructure that is far more sustainable, affordable, and holistic.

I also invest my time and resources into concepts such as social impact funds. In Chicago, 40 Acres Fresh Market is working to stop food insecurity and eliminate food deserts in underserved neighborhoods. They offer fresh and organic food through their mobile grocery store and their popup markets on the South Side and the West Side of Chicago.[16] This operation was made possible because of a social impact fund through the American Heart Association (AHA). The AHA realized they could help lower rates of cardiac issues and strokes by an intense focus on (1) improved community health, (2) access to healthcare resources (3) availability of fresh food and a realignment of social determinants of health, and (4) an awareness of the structural racism that prevents holistic care delivery.

A society is only as strong as its most disenfranchised citizens. Inequality and injustice are inextricably tied to the social determinants of health, which is why it is urgent that we act to improve the conditions in these communities. The privileged seem to finally be acknowledging these issues because awareness and empathy (being "woke") is fashionable these days. However, sudden empathy for these communities, much like the DEI efforts that I have seen since the murder of George Floyd, consists mainly of lip service. A mentor once told me that the difference between empathy and compassion is action. Like one of my favorite MCs, Redman, once wrote, it's "Time 4 Sum Aksion."

---

[1] "Key Moments in Flint, Michigan's Lead-Tainted Water Crisis," The Associated Press (January 12. 2021).
[2] *Narrative of the Life of Frederick Douglass, An American Slave*, by Frederick Douglass.
[3] "Black History Month: A Medical Perspective: Hospitals," Duke University Medical Center Library and Archives.
[4] "Racial Eugenics," Equal Justice Initiative (October 1, 2013).
[5] "About the USPHS Syphilis Study," Tuskegee University (tuskegee.edu/about-us/centers-of-excellence/bioethics-center/about-the-usphs-syphilis-study).
[6] "Systematic Inequality," by Angela Hanks, Danyelle Solomon, and Christian E. Weller, Center for American Progress (February 21, 2018).
[7] *Born a Crime: Stories From a South African Childhood*, by Trevor Noah (One World, 2016); page 73.
[8] *Stamped: Racism, Antiracism, and You*, by Jason Reynolds and Ibram X. Kendi (Little, Brown Books for Young Readers, 2020); page 253.
[9] *American Lion: Andrew Jackson in the White House*, by Jon Meacham (Random House, 2008); page 174.
[10] "The New Gilded Age," by Estelle Sommeiller and Mark Price, Economic Policy Institute (July 19, 2018).
[11] "How Can We Reduce Disparities in Health?" The Health Inequality Project.
[12] "The Association Between Income and Life Expectancy in the United States, 2001–2014," *Journal of American Medical Association* (April 26. 2016).
[13] "Stress in America: Paying With Our Health," American Psychological Association (February 4, 2015).
[14] "Stress and Health Disparities: Contexts, Mechanisms, and Interventions Among Racial/Ethnic Minorities and Low Socioeconomic Status Populations, American Psychological Association (2017).
[15] "How Can We Reduce Disparities in Health?"
[16] 40 Acres Fresh Market (fortyacresfreshmarket.com/about).

Chapter 3

A Healthy Assessment of the Pandemic, the Protests, and the Loss of Profit Within Health Care and Throughout the United States

"We need the harm to stop in our communities. We need the damage to be repaired. We need . . . to have a life of dignity, and the possibility to thrive," Opal Tometi, Co-founder, Black Lives Matter Movement

Covid and the color line are profound. Like slavery, it will haunt this country for years to come. Opal Tometi, a Black Lives Matter co-founder, references the unrest that took place during the summer of 2020 after the murder of George Floyd; but she could have been speaking to any of the three P's that have forever changed our country.

In many communities, the pandemic has disproportionately affected African Americans' access to improved health, sustained employment, and a better quality of life. The protests reflected Black people's cries for justice because of what routinely happens in our communities at the hands of the police. While unscrupulous industries continue to take advantage of people of color to increase their profits, the wealth gap widens between Black and white families.

HEALTHY DISRUPTION

These injustices remain interconnected, interwoven, and interspersed throughout nearly every major metropolis. Black people take menial service jobs, which predispose them to Covid and limit their profit-earning potential. Systemic and structural racism is in full effect while the three P's are omnipresent.

However, people are taking notice. The quarantine forced the country to take a hard look at what was happening not just in the streets of major US cities, but in cities and towns across the country and around the world. Activists mobilized for change and showed us how much protests have changed—or stayed the same—since the Civil Rights era. Unlike other eras, white people and the privileged were watching and joining in. Coalition-building starts organically, and the alignment of interests and outrage unites humanity. It does not happen often, but when it does, it is powerful.

The pandemic served as a wake-up call for the healthcare industry. Whether we will heed it is yet to be determined. The healthcare system is paid based on the number of people who receive care in hospitals. The system is even more lucrative when patients receive intensive care, as reimbursements are usually higher.

At the onset of Covid, we learned a valuable lesson about the fragility of the healthcare system. The industry discovered the truth that we were not as agile as we thought we were, and we are not as prepared for surges, no matter how many drills we have conducted in incident command. Because most hospitals in March 2020 were still concerned with volume and the industry was working to pack their hospitals, the devastation of Covid hit hard when intensive care unit (ICU) beds were most critical and patients with less-invasive illnesses were not in the ambulatory setting.

CHAPTER THREE

I see enormous opportunity in the aftermath of 2020, but it will take evolutionary leaders with revolutionary thinking to repair our broken industry. To expand that mindset, the healthcare system is a microcosm of our society, and we can ask ourselves some of the same questions we ask in the industry:

- How are we treating our patients?
- How are we treating our fellow citizens?
- How do we care for those who are on the margins?

The healthcare industry falls into the same trap that many physicians fall into. The industry's role is not necessarily to heal. The body does that naturally. Physicians, nurses, and practitioners can intervene on the body's behalf to help facilitate the healing process, but they do not have the power to heal. The industry's role is to empower patients to heal themselves.

From a mental health perspective, psychiatrists do not perform surgery or touch patients at all. They may prescribe medication. However, psychiatrists intercede, educate, and advocate for patients so that the opportunity for healing is clear to those patients receiving treatment.

Likewise, there are opportunities for the healthcare industry to do an intervention *to* the patient. The industry may go even further and do something *for* the patients. The platinum rule of health (not health care) stipulates that engagement and empowerment is top of mind, and we remind ourselves constantly that we should be administering care *with* the patient. Those on the front lines should be commended because they focused on the platinum rule consistently during the pandemic.

HEALTHY DISRUPTION

*****

The pandemic exposed the healthcare industry as dysfunctional. This level of exposure should motivate many healthcare leaders to shift into high gear and work to change an antiquated system where the patient is not empowered.

During the height of the pandemic, I watched many basketball games, and I learned that the NBA created a "bubble" location for players, coaches, staff, and the media. All of those within the bubble were tested regularly and could only interact with one another throughout the season. However, after the senseless shooting of a 29-year-old Black man by a police officer in Kenosha, Wisconsin, the NBA was the first of many leagues to "burst their bubble," so to speak.

The victim, Jacob Blake, was from my hometown of Milwaukee; and the Milwaukee Bucks read a statement after the shooting, indicating that they would not be playing their game that evening. The Bucks' organization stood in solidarity with the Blake family and were united as they read the statement. Many players then stepped outside the bubble to speak out about the consistent injustices throughout this country at the hands of police. Other leagues—including the WNBA, the MLB, and the NFL—also spoke out.

Before long, athletes from different areas of the sports world were unified for a cause sparked by a moment, creating momentum. This awareness led to a suspension of all sports across the country, and discussions began within all major league sports surrounding racial injustice and what to do about it.

Health care has been in a bubble for quite some time. Many leaders have not had the courage or the skill set to burst it. The insularity of our industry has led to insular thinking without acknowledgment

CHAPTER THREE

or any material change to the health and wealth of the communities we are fortunate to serve.

Although I was not thoroughly optimistic, I was hoping that the pandemic was going to serve as a catalyst for healthcare leaders to stand in solidarity for change, much like it was for athletes during the summer of 2020. Furthermore, I thought that breakthroughs in health research, such as the Covid vaccination, would stimulate a bubble-bursting effect. I was naïve to think that political proclivities would be eradicated for the safety of those in power and their communities. Instead, we seem to be enduring a time when the population is entrenched in various agendas, not necessarily based on fact, but insulated, much like the healthcare industry. For us to disrupt this industry and then unify around real solutions, we must burst our bubbles and step outside our silos, freeing ourselves and our minds.

COVID-19 gave the healthcare industry greater insight as to just how ill-equipped we are to deal with issues at scale. Healthcare leaders should be able to pivot quickly, move inside and outside of the hospital, and be able to message appropriately to the public. Solutions and execution during the onset of the pandemic were half-baked, and it displayed a discombobulated industry with misaligned motives.

The industry was caught off-guard because we did not use data and technology to our advantage. Healthcare leaders will often review historical data and work to predict what will occur in the health of entire populations. Unfortunately, this technique is applied among many sectors in health care: provider, payer, and pharmaceuticals. Health care is dynamic, and it is transient from person to person. Data and technology in real time could improve patient engagement, satisfaction, and outcomes.

HEALTHY DISRUPTION

This exposure to the issues within health care that the pandemic posed was actually valuable for the industry. The adage that "Necessity is the mother of invention" possibly held true for health care during the onset of the pandemic. However, it was Agatha Christie who stated, "I don't think necessity is the mother of invention. Invention, in my opinion, arises directly from idleness, possible also from laziness—to save oneself trouble."[1] Christie's comment on invention is more probable and apt as it relates to the current mentality of the healthcare industry.

The healthcare industry had all the data and technology that it is currently using at its fingertips for years, but it was too idle and perhaps too lazy to use it. The pandemic unmasked the problems around how specific communities received information and care. Health care was shoved unwillingly into the twenty-first century. Using data and technology, the industry maintained touch points with patients and outreach with communities that needed it most, especially the elderly and those persons with multiple chronic diseases. Even then, our lack of nimbleness created self-inflicted obstacles.

Policymakers did not relax the standards for intrastate telemedicine standards until the spring of 2020. Providers did not begin promoting telehealth until there were well over 250,000 deaths. This made a huge difference in patient outreach and being able to redirect those who did not need the ICU for other care options.

As a director on the board of a major telemedicine company and as a leader of a national health system that saw its telehealth visits increase over 700 percent during the first three months of Covid, I am an ardent advocate of marrying technology with health care. These technologies serve as a vehicle to accumulate more personal patient data that is germane for fostering customized care.

CHAPTER THREE

Social determinants of health, especially environmental factors, play a huge role in evaluating care. Typical healthcare services make up only about ten percent of a person's overall health and lifestyle. The other 90 percent are predicated on a person's access to healthy food, intake of accurate information (education gap and digital divide phenomena), and overall living conditions, for example. By sending healthcare providers into patients' homes to administer care, the provider can learn invaluable information about the patient: habits, surroundings, food and nutrition, and preferences for care.

These data are important to developing a customized care plan specifically for that patient. With this type of personal outreach, providers can adequately educate patients on nutrition and the importance of chronic disease management. This approach offers better preventative medicine and prescription drug adherence and mitigates a "cooker cutter" or population strategy and deployment to care.

Health care is reactive, and home health allows providers to be more proactive, using data that will be instrumental in holistically caring for patients who need that type of care. It also empowers patients on their own terms. Studies have shown that patients convalesce best and quicker when placed in environments that they know. The platinum rule (versus the Golden Rule) of humanity can be applied with a method such as home health within health care.

African Americans disproportionately suffer with chronic diseases, whether it is hereditary, lifestyle, or a deficit of a key element within the social determinants of health. The country's infrastructure that supports disparities within communities of color versus the privileged neighborhoods were never more glaring than during the pandemic. The CDC estimates that 34 percent of the deaths from Covid were among Black people, although we comprise only 12 percent of the population.

"In Chicago, residents in highly segregated neighborhoods with higher social vulnerability, such as high levels of poverty and lower levels of education, income, and employment, are disproportionately exposed to social and health risks. The intersection of factors was found to be associated with high death rates from COVID-19. Similarly, in a nationwide analysis, counties with higher population percentages (non-Hispanic) Black people experienced COVID-19 confirmed cases, hospitalizations, and death rates than counties with higher population percentages of (non-Hispanic) white people."[2]

I am frustrated that these disparities are not widely known, nor did healthcare institutions work to address issues that are only growing in number by the day. As stated, these issues are compounded by the fact that Black people have high rates of unemployment, are on the front lines in service industry job roles, and lack access to health care and equal circumstances surrounding social determinants of health.

Suddenly, at the onset of the pandemic, people of color were represented among essential workers. "Essential workers," code for persons who work for low wages, were heroes because they were doing the jobs the rest of us were not willing to do. Though they were surely underpaid for the long hours and hard work, they could be found doing the service jobs, including jobs in the healthcare industry, which led to a loss of profit-earning potential as well as higher susceptibility to Covid.

I am also baffled that the Surgeon General, the CDC, and other healthcare agencies did not shout from the mountaintops the importance of proper sleep, exercise, and diet. We heard more about

CHAPTER THREE

President Donald Trump's unfounded assertions about bleach in the blood and the medications Remdesivir and Regeneron than we did about the importance of proper fuel for the body. We rarely discuss the indescribable marvel of the American diet.

There have been a myriad of studies on diet tied to health, but there has not been much intervention. There have not been many incentives from payers to relax premiums for those who eat healthfully. There are plenty of incentives for smoking cessation, but not for healthy eating. I admired the effort from First Lady Michelle Obama in her Let's Move campaign and tying it to gardening and fresh foods, but I was bewildered when she was vilified for it and why more Black people did not support the movement. From an overall health perspective, I am not convinced that Americans—Black or white–want to be healthy.

The CDC, Dr. Anthony Fauci, and the National Institute of Allergy and Infectious Disease estimated that between 130,000 and 210,000 Covid-related deaths could have been prevented during the first six months of the disease. I agreed with their citing of public awareness, social distancing, masking, and proper personal hygiene as methods to help mitigate the virus. However, I would go further and state that many of those who died were suffering for mismanagement of chronic diseases such as constructive obstructive pulmonary disease (COPD), chronic heart failure, and obesity.

In 2020, the CDC estimates that roughly 42.4 percent of Americans are considered obese, a 26 percent increase since 2008. It is estimated that over 500,000 Americans per year die due to obesity and poor diet.[3] About 48 percent of all African Americans are clinically obese, and of that 48 percent, nearly 57 percent are Black women.[4] These staggering statistics among Americans and Black people are part in parcel to the growing issues surrounding deprivation of sound and equal social determinants of health.

However, in large part, the significance of poor eating habits and penitent food choices are the elementary issue leading to these statistics. This is not about body shaming. This is about bringing awareness to a crisis, a crisis that could have led to fewer deaths during the pandemic. Covid is a pandemic, and obesity is reaching epidemic proportions in this country; but those problems could be mitigated beginning with proper diet.

As having been recently diagnosed with diabetes and chronic kidney disease, I have never been more aware of the power of good nutrition and how it affects my body. The incidence of chronic disease for African Americans is 11 times higher than that of our white counterparts among adults. The prevalence of multiple chronic diseases is a woeful 14 times higher.[5] The disparities are evident that it seemingly leads to Black people's ability to establish and obtain generational wealth due to our health-related concerns.

There were many in this country and around the world who are personally affected by COVID-19. I lost two family members to the pandemic in March and April of 2020. As if it were not hitting home already, given my chosen profession, losing people close to me made it that much more real. Both of my family members were enduring chronic diseases, and sadly their conditions were probably mismanaged by their respective families and the healthcare system. Because of their zip codes, they lacked basic access to health care, food, information, and education. They lived in conditions that were subpar at best and infested with other infectious diseases at worst.

The pandemic hit the disenfranchised and the vulnerable first and the hardest at a tender time in this country. This also led to a chronic

CHAPTER THREE

disease that plagues many communities of color, given the conditions we withstand in the country: mental health instability.

Dating back to slavery, mental health issues carry a stigma that drives many Black people to internalize their feelings and not seek professional help. We do not lean into our various networks and family members, and we may feel that we are facing our problems alone. This has been tragically exacerbated over the last year. "During the pandemic, about 4 in 10 adults in the US have reported symptoms of anxiety or depressive disorder, a share that has been largely consistent [throughout the pandemic], up from 1 and 10 adults in 2019 [prior to the pandemic]."[6]

These statistics refer only to those Americans who report their issues. Unlike the Covid death toll, there was not much, if any, data delineating mental health reports among races in America. Perhaps, many of us are still not seeking care, given the long-term historical stigma mental health treatment has had for many Black people.

Our social norms must also be studied and revamped as we continue to evaluate the spread of Covid. Currently, Congress and President Joe Biden are working to pass an infrastructure bill that will address dilapidated structures throughout the country. I am hopeful that air filtration, HEPA filters, and other helpful resources will be common in the future to ensure that buildings are not only safe, but have proper recyclable air that is needed to lessen the instances of disease transmission, especially in places such as schools and airports.

Also, Americans must not overlook the need for overall distance from other human beings in general. More than 83 percent of the country's population live in metropolitan areas, and these crowded cities continue to grow each year. Space is at a premium and is more

HEALTHY DISRUPTION

valuable now than ever before. As we understand how communicable diseases are transmitted, the healthcare industry has an opportunity to emphasize social distancing and personal hygiene to keep populations safe. This is where the big P of population health should be implemented swiftly.

Finally, the vaccination argument rages on. Data, facts, and science should prevail, which led to the development of the Covid vaccines so quickly. Similar to how our country operates, health care rarely reinvents the wheel; rather, it innovates based on what is already established. The Covid vaccination was based on previous work after the SARS outbreak in February 2003. Unfortunately, this was not communicated well.

Messaging should have been clear, concise, and unified, but there was a failure to galvanize and rally people around the cause for vaccination for the sake of humanity. Also the tools to mobilize the message were poorly implemented. Unfortunately, about 50 to 60 percent of Americans are vaccinated, and we have hovered around that number for quite some time since the initial surge in vaccinations. It is estimated that about 40 percent of the country still holds conspiracy theories against the vaccine. Many of these theories have emanated from QAnon/MAGA/Trump supporters and not Black people, which is ironic since we as a group have endured many issues involving clandestine experimentation and substandard medicine in this country.

Health care, the United States, and the world are still coping with the pandemic as it continues to explode. Learning is always acceptable, but the failure to allow science, data, and technology to enable sound decision-making and prudent choices is not.

CHAPTER THREE

*****

In *The Tempest*, William Shakespeare wrote, "What's past is prologue," and it seems as though we are living through history. The protests of 2020 may seem more vivid, given our 24-hour news cycle and the impact of social media, but structural and systemic racism, critical race theory, oppression, wealth gaps, policy brutality, war, and social injustice are not novel. Conversely, one could argue that social media has bought these issues into the social consciousness of America as at no other time. Regrettably, the social consciousness awakens in this country when the privileged are embarrassed.

General David Hurley said, "The standard you walk by is the standard you accept." The privileged have accepted the standard of police brutality to Black people since slavery. Enslaved Africans were beaten by overseers for no apparent reason. Instead of the overseers' overalls, those who beat us now wear blue uniforms. Today, one of the major differences is that the brutality is in the faces of Americans because we were forced to be at home during the pandemic. Although America's social consciousness was awakened, Black people's consciousness is always awake.

This forced agitation from society is often dismissed by the privileged as paranoia, but for me, it has become a way of life, personally and professionally. Social media just pushed the narrative to quickly mobilize and to shame the privileged. When the streets exploded in protests after the murder of George Floyd, justice needed boots on the ground, not just keyboard warriors. For too long, people in the healthcare industry and across the country have been passive in their participation to bring about equity, equality, justice, and inclusion. The protests exposed who was willing to take to the streets and those who were satisfied to stay behind the scenes and their screens.

HEALTHY DISRUPTION

Malcolm X said, "You don't stick a knife in a man's back nine inches and then pull it out six inches and say you're making progress." Professing support for a movement is not the same as making actual progress to equality within our broken systems. We still have much work to do.

In their book, *Stamped: Racism, Antiracism, and You*, Jason Reynolds and Ibram X. Kendi scold those who leave the heavy lifting to those willing to protest: "Scrolling will never be enough. Reposting will never be enough. Hashtagging will never be enough. . . . All of us—have to fight against performance and lean into participation. We must be participants. Active. We must be more than audience members sitting comfortably in the stands. . . . That's too easy. Instead, we must be players on the field, on the court, in our classrooms and communities, trying to do right. Because it takes a whole hand—both hands—to grab hold of hatred. Not just a texting thumb and a scrolling index finger."[7]

In the summer of 2020, I marched alongside many people whom I had never met nor probably will see again. I marched as I traveled for work. In any city that was conducting a protest, I joined in. I marched in Chicago, Cincinnati, Atlanta, Miami, and Memphis. I even took my daughter to one of the protests in Kenosha, Wisconsin, after the police shooting of Jacob Black because it hit home for me.

I met activists, athletes, entrepreneurs, businesspeople, and others who chose health care as a profession. I saw the power of a unified front, felt the energy of a collective spirit, and heard the pain of oppression from past generations. It was a sight to see not necessarily for me, but for the privileged who had no idea and did not see color. They definitely saw it when I was protesting because we had the courage to confront long-lasting and painful issues in the country.

CHAPTER THREE

Confrontation is needed to transform a flawed and perplexing system aimed at providing cover to the privileged. Confrontation can serve as the mirror and the wake-up call to action.

The word *confrontation* can have a negative—even violent—connotation. *Confrontation* is defined as "to face and deal with boldly and directly." For me, confrontation is our opportunity to finally deal with what has been ailing us as a country and in the healthcare industry for years. Confrontation is the fastest vehicle for change. It exploits the incongruence of humanity but also congers the crux of human behavior for the need of acceptance, regardless of viewpoint. By definition, neither Americans nor healthcare leadership have been bold or direct. Instead, we have been stuck in the status quo, which has led to meaningless platitude exchanges and inaction.

The roll call of those who have been victims of police brutality seems to be growing. We have heard the names of Sandra Bland, Ahmaud Arbery, Breonna Taylor, George Floyd, and Rayshard Books—among others. Many of the Black people who have suffered such brutality were going about their daily lives: jogging, hanging out in the neighborhood, sleeping at home, or eating a meal. I have done all of these things, so I could have been targeted and killed just as easily.

However, let us not forget those who were beaten by the police and lived to tell about it. Rodney King and yours truly come to mind. However, after Floyd was murdered, the outcry was, "Say their names!" When training staff members to effectively interact with patients, we tell them to do the same: Say their names. To be transparent, it is a tactic we use to increase patient satisfaction scores, but it also demonstrates humanity and elicits a response from the patient that is often engaging. During the protests, however, the difference was that the people's names we were chanting were dead at the hands of police. In the two weeks after Floyd was murdered in May 2020, more than 2,000 protests were held across all 50 states.

As we were leaving the Kenosha protests, my 12-year-old daughter asked what more could she do? Immediately, I thought of Darnella Frazier. Frazier was 17 years old when she caught the murder of Floyd on video. She said that as she was capturing the video, she did not know what to do. She felt helpless because she knew Floyd was dying and that she could not save his life. She said Floyd's death would change her life forever.

The following year, Frazier showed tremendous growth and perspective. She eloquently said, "Even though this was a traumatic life-changing experience for me, I'm proud of myself. If it weren't for my video, the world wouldn't have known the truth. I own that. My video didn't save George Floyd, but it put his murderer away and off the streets."[8]

I think we can all harness a little of Frazier's spirit. We may not know exactly what to do, but we can do something. I often wonder what would happen in the healthcare industry and across the country if we all adopted that notion. Do something, because doing nothing is not an option anymore. If you examine the sentiment, Frazier indicated that she, along with Floyd, changed the world. She did it because she was not afraid to capture the truth. I try to share that same outlook with my daughter.

Frankly, Frazier's video forced a nation to see what it did not want to see. When Americans and people around the world saw the raw truth before us, it haunted us and spurred some people to action. The privileged were embarrassed, and many of them said, "We have

CHAPTER THREE

to do something about this." For the first time in a long time, people from all walks of life were paying attention. According to Jon Meacham, the power is in seeing: "When the nation sees differently, it enhances its capacity to act differently. From Seneca Falls to Selma to Stonewall, America has gradually expanded who's included when the country speaks of 'We the People.'"[9]

Conversely, I was awestruck by what I witnessed on January 6, 2021. An angry mob stormed the Capital building in Washington, DC, after President Donald Trump gave a speech inciting a feeling of fear. This type of fear was based on conjecture that somehow the privileged were losing this country and they had to take back America. There are so many racial undertones in the type of rhetoric. Moreover, the MAGA slogan, "Make America Great Again," was not inherently racist until the word *again* was added.

Many American citizens would love to make America great, but when the Trump campaign added the word *again*, it implied that America was once great and must return to its greatness. Further, Black people equate the nostalgia and longing for yesteryear that is embedded in the MAGA slogan as a return to slavery or, at the very least, Jim Crow. Given the invasion of the Capitol building, it served as another wake-up call to the privileged that the Far Right will go to great lengths to uphold white supremacy.

Within a span of less than six months, there is not a more interesting and stark juxtaposition of protests. With the BLM protests, which were mostly peaceful, there was a group fighting to gain equality and justice. With the MAGA protest, where many were injured and several died, it was a group fighting to keep their way of life.

HEALTHY DISRUPTION

Subsequent to the protest, one of the outcries for justice centered on police training and resources. There were calls for defunding the police, but that message got lost in translation. A better interpretation of what is needed, especially in marginalized communities, is a diverse team of people who come alongside the police and offer services that our law enforcement officers have never been trained to deliver. Some of the budget pumped into police departments could be better spent on social services and community development.

While we should always be evaluating our municipal, county, and state budgets, this latest rally cry hearkened back to health care for two reasons: (1) The sentiment was sound, but the message was flawed, similar to the ACA rollout. There should have been a consideration of funds that were extracted from some of the municipalities. *The New York Times* reported in June 2020 that less than four percent of police intervention turns violent and is criminal. It is usually routine and can be deescalated by the time the police arrive. (2) It serves as an opportunity for municipalities to break out of their insular thinking and partner with other community outfits (social work, private businesses). Health care has the opportunity to do the same.

Whether it is the police department, social workers, local and state officials, or corporations who put their money where their mouth is and partner with our communities, we need allies who will come into our communities and help facilitate change. Before becoming doctors, medical students take the Hippocratic Oath. Part of that oath says, "First, do no harm." I think those who pledge to protect and serve could align themselves with that vow.

Whether it occurs through a murder caught on video, microaggressions in the office or at school, low wages for essential workers, lack of access to housing, food deserts, or an abundance of

CHAPTER THREE

opportunities to garner guns and drugs, we have had more harm done than good in our communities in the last 20 months and beyond. It is pervasive and structural and benefits the privileged.

*****

More people reached the billionaire status in 2020 and 2021 during the pandemic than anytime in this country's history. Existing billionaires increased their wealth on average by 15 percent. The top four corporations (Amazon, Apple, Google, and Microsoft) leaped into one fifth of the GDP by themselves—over 21 percent. That equates to more than all of health care within the economy. Meanwhile, small businesses closed, and medium-sized businesses weakened by way of revenue and profit.

Consequently, the food stamp benefit jumped 27 percent compared to pre-pandemic proportions.[10] I would have thought that a recession, if not a financial depression, was upon us, given such a global pandemic in our midst. However, this pandemic has exposed yet another ugly truth in the United States: The rich usually get richer during crises, and the poor get nothing.

A Pew Research Center survey found that overall, 25 percent of US adults say they or someone in their household has been laid off or lost jobs because of the coronavirus outbreak, with young adults (ages 18-29) and lower-income adults among the most likely to say this has occurred in their household. Of those who said they personally lost jobs, half of them said they are still unemployed as of the summer of 2021. Lower-income adults who were laid off due to the coronavirus are less likely to be working now than middle- and upper-income adults who lost their jobs: 43 percent versus 58 percent, respectively.

HEALTHY DISRUPTION

As city and state officials ordered lockdowns and quarantines, businesses that were not considered essential had to close. Many of these businesses closed for months, and they opened up toward the end of the year. Others closed, never to open again. Many of these were small mom-and-pop businesses that could not remain closed and compete with the big box stores that remained open. Entrepreneurs saw all their hard work evaporate in a matter of months, and many of these business owners had no idea what would come next.

Pew also reports that Americans who have experienced job or wage loss, personally or in their household, are more than twice as likely as those who have not to say they have had trouble paying their bills, struggled to pay their rent or mortgage, used money from savings or retirement to pay bills, or borrowed money from friends or family.[11]

By June 2020, as many as 7.7 million workers had lost jobs with employer-sponsored insurance because of the COVID-19 pandemic, and these health plans covered 6.9 million dependents as well.[12] Estimates are that during the last three quarters of 2020, on average, about a third of those who lost employer-sponsored insurance (ESI) coverage through pandemic-related job loss will become uninsured. About a third will obtain coverage through another family member's ESI, just over a quarter will become covered by Medicaid or the Children's Health Insurance Program (CHIP), and a small percentage will obtain nongroup insurance.[13]

Although jobs are being created quarter over quarter, the uninsured population has grown exponentially over the last year due to unemployment and underemployment. Many employers are no longer offering benefits to their employees, and people are working

CHAPTER THREE

two or three jobs to pay bills. Health insurance is often not a priority during these difficult days.

I do not think we have even begun to scratch the surface on how deep these issues are. The pandemic has highlighted the fact that these issues will continue to grow. Healthcare leaders, policymakers, and payers should support the ACA on its merits and help the enrollment and proliferation of it for better outcomes.

After President Biden's initial $2 trillion Covid rescue and relief plan, the United States would have pumped over $5 trillion into the economy since March 2020. Unfortunately, many people received their stimulus checks, but communities of color have not benefited from the $5 trillion price tag. Based on statistics, the inverse is probably true for the privileged.

As I examined the role profit has played in all of this, I wanted to shift my focus away from money and to something far more important. Profit goes well beyond corporate earnings, the Dow, or the GDP. Profit also includes people and their ability to earn a living during and after this pandemic.

I have neighbors, friends, family members, fellow church members, and patients who could not afford to miss a paycheck before the pandemic. Now, they are in even worse financial shape. They wonder if they will be evicted during this time of economic uncertainty. Essential workers often do not have the luxury of working from home or switching to a better-paying job during the pandemic. Instead, they have to expose themselves to Covid daily, as well as to racial injustice to take on the work that is critical so the privileged in this country can continue to thrive.

What profit looks like to me is human dignity and respect. Prosperity is rooted in the African sentiment of *Sankofa*: I am because we are. But we have lost that spirit of community and communal care. We have turned inward and become more self-centered and comfortable with our own wealth and privilege. Instead of growing the pie so that we all get bigger slices, we have focused on the current size of the pie and tried to cut one another out to get a larger piece.

*****

"We're all in this together." How many times have we heard that during the pandemic, protests against social injustice, and economic woes? At times, this statement feels more like a hope than a reality.

It is fitting that the biggest health crisis of our time, which is spurring the most severe economic devastation in decades, has led to what is likely the most prolific protests ever for racial justice. The pain and anguish from the pandemic and the need to protest to invoke social change is palpable. The confluence of the three P's of the pandemic, protests, and loss of profit are the impetus for emotion, controversy, and disparity.

After the events of 2020, I felt compelled to examine pandemic, protests, and profit individually to question our station as a nation, what we learned or missed, and how we can improve. Since health care is related to everything in life, it did not surprise me to see that common thread running throughout.

But 2020 showed us that we can recalibrate so we can get into alignment. Even a small misalignment compounds over time and becomes much more severe. We have been misaligned for so long. We need to find harmony as defined when "your head, your heart, your gut, and your feet are all going in the same direction." We need to create harmony, not just within ourselves, but within our communities and within the country we are working to build for the next generation.

CHAPTER THREE

During the confluence of these unfortunate events, I have learned so much. I have taken on the mantle of tackling an antiquated and racist industry within a racist country, but the anguish and anxiety make that mantle heavy. Throughout the pandemic, I often heard the axiom "This is the new normal." I would argue that a normal cannot be new and that there was never a normal in the first place. The realization of the "no normal" is upon us, and those who can deal with change will be the better for it.

---

[1] *Agatha Christie: An Autobiography*, by Agatha Christie, reprint edition (William Morrow Paperbacks, 2010).
[2] The Centers for Disease Control and Prevention, National Center for Health Statistics (December 2020).
[3] *The Journal of the American Medical* Association (2020).
[4] *The American Psychological Association* (2020).
[5] The Centers for Disease Control and Prevention.
[6] Kaiser Family Foundation (February 2021).
[7] *Stamped: Racism, Antiracism, and You*, by Jason Reynolds and Ibram X. Kendi (Little Brown Books for Young Readers, 2020); page 253.
[8] "Read This Powerful Statement From Darnella Frazier, Who Filmed George Floyd's Murder," by Joe Hernandez, NPR (May 26, 2021).
[9] *His Truth Is Marching On: John Lewis and the Power of Hope*, by Jon Meacham (Random House, 2020); page 12.
[10] *The Washington Post* (2021).
[11] "Economic Fallout From COVID-19 Continues to Hit Lower-Income Americans the Hardest," by Kim Parker, Rachel Minkin, Jesse Bennett, Pew Research Center (September 24, 2020).
[12] "How Many Americans Have Lost Jobs With Employer Health Coverage During the Pandemic?" by Paul Fronstin and Steven A. Woodbury, The Commonwealth Fund (October 1, 2020).
[13] "Changes in Health Insurance Coverage Due to the COVID-19 Recession, by Jessica Banthin, Michael Simpson, Matthew Buettgens, Linda J. Blumberg, Robin Wang, Urban Institute (July 13, 2020).

Chapter 4

Creating a Healthy Platform for Change

"Change won't come from the top. Change will come from mobilized grassroots."
President Barack Obama, Dreams From My Father: A Story of Race and Inheritance

Mike Tyson once haphazardly stated, "Everybody has got a plan until they get punched in the mouth." In 2020, the United States and the healthcare industry got "punched in the mouth." Enduring the pandemic, coming to terms with America's social injustice issues, and the immersive loss of profit in the country and throughout healthcare entities certainly exposed warts that were overlooked or purposely concealed, particularly for the marginalized.

Health care is a microcosm of society, and the political and social health of the nation usually closely mirrors what is transpiring in the society at large. If we look back at significant events and major policies in the United States, the health and well-being of the least advantaged has been adversely affected.

HEALTHY DISRUPTION

"For African Americans, the average annual cost for healthcare premiums is almost 20 percent of the average household income compared to 10 percent of a white family—a major cost to bear when taking into account the income inequality and other economic challenges for this demographic."[1]

*****

Although injustices have been exposed in various forms since slavery, it was not until the mid-twentieth century that the United States began to feel the winds of change. Activists from many walks of life marched and protested. Like the protests of 2020 after the murder of George Floyd, many Americans from other races, creeds, and nationalities started to recognize the plight of African Americans and decided to work with them for change.

Consequently, it was the prudence and astuteness of Dr. Martin Luther King Jr. that made a connection that I also assert. In Chicago in 1966, King gave a speech at the Convention of the Medical Committee for Human Rights. As part of his plea to Americans in regards to the Poor People's Campaign, he said that inequity in health care is the worst form of injustice.

During the Civil Rights Movement of the 1960s, there was tremendous advancement that was realized, despite the assassinations of Black leaders that stymied the spirit, thought, and equality of African Americans. Bills were passed, schools and public places were integrated, and Black businesses were created in the name of equality. However, the lack of true transformative and sustained change during the 1960s was not as much about health care as it was about the health and social injustices that Black people had to endure.

They saw the disparities, but they lacked the concern to fix them or they did not have the resources to alleviate them. Civil rights

CHAPTER FOUR

activists realized that the powerful and the privileged could change the system but would remain unfazed by the suffering of others. They deliberately and strategically made sure that the disparities between white and Black, rich and poor, were continued into the future.

After intense study of the Civil Rights Movement, I came to admire the resourcefulness and mobilization efforts of Black people during that era. I hold two fundamental perspectives on this period. First, partnership and coalition-building efforts among other like-minded, disenfranchised groups would have accelerated the introduction of legislation and the realization of the privileged to take notice as well.

It is unclear to me how some of the privileged are just not aware of injustices that have plagued our country for generations and that they are the beneficiaries of that injustice. This was the sea change after the murder of George Floyd because the world was watching due to the pandemic. Often, it is up to those who are disadvantaged to shine a bright light on the disparities. I firmly believe that the assassinations of civil rights leaders like King and Fred Hampton only occurred when the coalition-building efforts became wildly adopted by others outside the Black race. For King and Hampton, it was the poor and their oppression and the Latin community in Chicago, respectively.

Second, the privileged also recognize and are threatened by the accumulation of land and wealth. If there was an opportunity not only to partner, but to purchase land and businesses during the Civil Rights Era, it would have been even more potent and would have withstood the power struggle that was sure to ensue by way of new policies to keep people of color oppressed.

HEALTHY DISRUPTION

In the 1980s, the oppression became more strategic and covert under the Reagan administration. President Ronald Reagan introduced a series of cuts that would decimate social service programs and increase unemployment levels. African Americans, who struggled to access quality health care, employment, and other essential services, were disproportionately affected by these eliminations.

Healthcare access was even more elusive as Medicaid lost 18 percent of its expenditures. The Department of Health and Human Services eliminated 25 percent of its budget, resulting in the loss of many public health and social services most needed in poor and marginalized communities.[2] These programmatic changes, along with government interventions such as COINTELPRO, which flooded Black communities in major cities with drugs, further exacerbated the Black plight in America and widened the financial chasm between Black and white families like never before.

Even children were adversely affected by the administration's slashing of health service budgets. Many of the programs that were established to help families feed their children and provide health care were cut. Unfortunately, "there was also an increase in preventable childhood diseases in poor populations." Half a million people could no longer receive Aid to Families With Dependent Children. One million people were denied food stamps, and 250 community health centers were closed. One million schoolchildren were no longer allowed to buy reduced-price lunches, and the funding for the Women, Infants, and Children (WIC) program was cut by two thirds.[4]

Reagan's cuts also negatively impacted employment for African Americans. The administration boasted a 55 percent increase in employment for Black people. Since many were employed by social

CHAPTER FOUR

welfare programs, which were drastically reduced in the administration's cuts, there would be a "higher percentage of Black people than whites to lose their jobs."[4] These unprecedented policy phenomena purposefully set the stage, spring-boarding Black people into a state of crime, drugs, and poverty.

*****

Health care is my ministry. It is not a profession for me, but more of a calling and the only way I know how to affect social change in America. When I initially entered the healthcare industry, I had a grand vision of what I could do for the underserved communities while making money. I think this desire emanated from witnessing my own family struggle during the Reagan era. However, I quickly learned that I was naive about the industry I was drawn to.

When I first felt called to work in health care, my dream was to return to Milwaukee or Chicago and turn the healthcare system on its head. I wanted to make sure family members and others in my community who desperately needed access to health care could improve their health and the quality of their lives. I wanted to build clinics in those forgotten communities; partner with churches to open more avenues to improved spirit, mind, and body health; and proliferate concepts such as federally qualified health centers (FQHC).

In retrospect, I have been fortunate enough to have achieved some of these goals, but I had to fight like hell to do so because health care is regulated, policy-driven, stagnant, and complacent. In addition, health care is one of the few industries that administers its product (care), and subsequently the people and institutions providing the care are reimbursed. This ass-backward approach only widens the gap for those who struggle for access and creates further issues surrounding the ability to pay for those who are disenfranchised.

HEALTHY DISRUPTION

Unfortunately, there is no incentive to change this practice because it is lucrative for major insurance companies, employers, and providers. Health care is big business but operates like a cottage industry. I have learned that working within a failed industry rests on my ability to monetize and capitalize concepts. This is what drew me to the investment side of health care several years ago.

Between my junior and senior years at Morehouse, I was inducted into one of the first cohorts for an internship with the Institute for Diversity in Healthcare Management. The Institute's mission is to "expand leadership opportunities for ethnic minorities in health services management. . . . [and] increase the number of minorities in health services administration to better reflect the increasingly diverse communities they serve."[5]

During that time, I was fortunate to shadow the chief operating officer of a large academic medical center in Omaha, Nebraska. To say that changed my life is an understatement. My eyes, my ears, and my spirit were awakened to the possibilities in health care, and it shifted my mindset. Initially, I wanted to pursue a career in medicine, become a physician, and follow in the footsteps of one of my first mentors. I learned that there is an implicit hierarchy in health care, and I was under the impression that I could impact the industry more fervently as a doctor. However, during my internship, everything changed.

As I worked closely with the hospital COO, I watched him preside over a system that he had no power to change. He ran into silos, roadblocks, territorial issues, and big egos. And that is what made me want to shake up the whole system. I was thrown into negotiations with physicians on a myriad of issues, and I learned that they did not have any real authority either. The total misalignment of physician

CHAPTER FOUR

incentives and the metrics that executives were rewarded for was on display, and that made me frustrated and dismayed. In my naïveté and zeal, I thought I could find ways to integrate more in one area and accelerate the work in other areas.

Because of what I had experienced during my internship, I thought it would be wise to minor in business. That shift led to a career I did not even know existed at the time, but it also led to the exposure of a lot of tough terrain and turmoil because I was being called into an industry that was so incredibly broken.

Instead of working from an individualized perspective like physicians, I thought I could impact the industry by healing the masses. It was for this reason that I decided against going the doctor track. In the harsh light of reality, my dreams of being a community doctor, helping to heal patients one by one, seemed ineffective and would be a slower approach to affecting change.

Consequently, I have learned that specificity within health care is sorely needed and is overlooked. Creating personalized care plans, focusing on one zip code, addressing one chronic disease type, and working to influence one social determinant of health are all opportunities in the healthcare arena. While this may take longer to realize change, it has proven to be more effective at addressing persistent issues, especially among the marginalized.

As a Black man in America, I know the value of time. Tomorrow is not promised for anyone, but for African Americans, it is far more critical to work to impact the world. Countless Black leaders have seen their efforts tragically cut short and have been killed while managing a movement, imprisoned for something they said, wrongly accused of a crime, or disparaged to the point that credibility becomes an issue. This is not only true for Black leaders in this

HEALTHY DISRUPTION

country, but these concepts are invoked into a supposedly altruistic industry like health care on a smaller scale for Black leaders as well.

I have worked to integrate the "The LeBron James Doctrine" into my life and career. As an avid basketball fan, I have been inspired by players such as LeBron James, Kevin Garnett, and Kobe Bryant, who circumvented college and went straight to the pros. As James has said, "You have to move while you have the muscle." This philosophy certainly angers many of the privileged who promote a "You have to pay your dues before you are allowed to lead" type of perspective. This archaic principle could not be more apparent in an industry like health care and is adopted by Black leaders who push it as religion to the millennials and future generations.

As a son of a former teacher and psychologist, I certainly support the power of education, but I do know that school is more so about training and less about education. Education comes through perspective, and that is now always promoted in school. So I did not want to spend almost a decade completing medical school, an internship, and a residency. That is not what the healthcare industry needed. It needed a shakeup—a disruption—and I wanted to place myself in the best position at the right time to do just that.

The bottom line is that no matter how frustrated I may be at this industry, I still have to do the hard work of self-reflection to become more self-aware. It would be hard to be an agent of change externally in the things that affect other people if I did not master the change I needed to do within. Through constant reflection and soul searching, which is still occurring, I discovered three things.

First, I am more anxious than ever. I have been extremely fortunate and have had success through hard work, compared to my white counterparts. However, I am in constant fear of losing it and being

CHAPTER FOUR

penalized for it, particularly by those in perceived roles of authority. I am more anxious now than when I was broke and had nothing. Most privileged people would diagnose me as paranoid, but I am confident that most Black leaders view this as normal and necessary.

Second, speaking of diagnoses, I realize that I suffer from two distinct issues: survivor's guilt and the disease to please. Survivor's guilt occurs when a person has feelings of remorse because they have benefited from a traumatic experience and others have not. I had many losses in my life: my best friend and countless relatives. For many African Americans, this too is commonplace because our ancestors and previous generations had to fight so hard for everything that they received. I am only three generations removed from slavery, and it breaks my heart that my great-grandfather probably could not fathom the opportunities that I have been given and my current station in life.

The disease to please has also plagued me for much of my life. The disease to please is often inherent for many Black people as it stems from our tribal and communal nature back in Africa. This weighs heavy for many Black leaders as they achieve success and feel the need to share and support others along their trajectory. These diseases eat at the core of Black leaders' mental stability and affect our opportunities to build, find, and sustain empowerment unless we acknowledge and forgive ourselves as we lead.

Third, I had to own my complicity in why things have not changed fast enough. It was painful, but coming to this conclusion has freed me to be intentional about encouraging like-minded people in the industry to affect change on every level.

It has also made me want to pour into the next generation the principles of investing, owning, and becoming entrepreneurs inside and outside health care with radical precision and execution. These concepts have been elusive to many Black leaders and have been purposefully withheld by the privileged who adopt a fixed mindset (versus a growth mindset) that stipulates they lose when other groups are realizing their fair share. These principles are pervasive in the industry and in this country.

Ostensibly, I am confident that most leaders have conducted much self-reflection. Like many organizations, I developed a personal mission statement, and I have examined all the areas in which I can be a change agent to uplift and inspire others: "By being the best version of a man I can elevate, advocate, support, and promote my family and friends and the Black plight and struggle in America, while providing information and access to the masses to ensure that marginalized populations have opportunities for economic, social, and cultural empowerment."

In many instances, I have seen where the browbeating is routine and learned behavior from previous generations, particularly within health care. However, accountability rests on leaders' ability to relate, understand, and appreciate the motivations of the people they are entrusted to lead. This is even more true for Black people as the public flogging mentality often invoked by the privileged is reminiscent of a slave master's or an overseer's treatment of our ancestors. As during slavery, this method is used to control and to aggrandize people who need to feed their own ego and feel more powerful. This type of abuse disincentivizes many Black people in the workplace and certainly serves as a reminder of exclusion often not acknowledged in any DEI effort.

*****

Health care is a $4 trillion-dollar industry, nearly 20 percent of the nation's gross domestic product (GDP). Unlike other industries

CHAPTER FOUR

that sell a tangible product, like Microsoft sells software and computer products, the healthcare industry's product is life. We are supposed to be making people feel better, saving people's lives. That is what I have always led with, but I have been disappointed that so many in the healthcare industry put profit over compassion, their bottom line over people. The healthcare industry is a two-sided beast: There is the business side and the care side, and both are broken.

This industry has a chronic illness. Others have acknowledged it as well, but there is a scarcity of people who are working to disrupt it. There are two major reasons for the healthcare industry's incrementalism:

1. The business side of the industry is siloed and sectorized. Industry leaders and organizations have constructed these silos to protect their own self-interest and profits. There are five major sectors within health care: patients, payers (insurance companies and health plans), pharmaceutical (drug companies), policymakers (government), and providers (doctors and hospitals).

2. The industry's insular approach is readily apparent when incentives are revealed. All five sectors possess and protect different incentives. This misalignment leads to a lack of willingness to partner with other sectors, higher costs, and lower quality of care throughout the industry.

3. The profit-earning potential is in the medicine not the cure. The overall industry is still incentivized on administering the most care possible and then in turn getting paid for whatever they said they did. This has facilitated a perpetual prescribing

of unnecessary drugs (which can lead to additions), unnecessary procedures, and more expense. Thus, the unnecessary care for some has not reached those who need it, causing wide disparities most deeply felt in minority and impoverished communities.

Unfortunately, the industry cannot move forward because it is unable to unlearn certain limited perspectives and stale theories on how to fix a healthcare system rooted in America dogma.

While I believe in using revolutionary tactics, I try to practice evolutionary thinking. Change agents need to be *flexible* instead of compromising or acquiescent. Those resistant to change become brittle over time, and no industry can evolve and grow if it is not nimble enough to adjust. *Diversified knowledge* is the antithesis of the siloed approach. Having a broader knowledge of the industry is a recipe for growth and change. *Ownership and responsibility* go hand in hand to gain internal and external trust. Those we serve will respect our willingness to take accountability and hold ourselves responsible for our performance.[6] I have learned that change agents often adopt a similar philosophy to remain focused, manage expectations, and maintain their sanity.

Dr. King espoused that leaders' purpose and influence is uncovered when they can answer an urgent and fundamental question: What have I done for others? At the end of every day, I ask myself, Who have I helped today? The metric reverberates in my head as I try to sleep.

Reaching back as I climb has always been a mantra and a leadership principle for me. I have the high honor of mentoring several people, and I am proud that they are stepping into their own in an

CHAPTER FOUR

industry I have devoted my life to. I am even more proud that all of them are also mentoring the next generation of leaders.

As much as I encourage those already in the industry to be agents of change where they are, it is the next generation I want to reach. That is where the change is going to happen. Unfortunately, the more seasoned health executives are not going to turn our industry upside down nor tear it down and work to build it back better. It will be the millennials and Generation Z that will radicalize and revolutionize the administration of and access to health care. When I talk to the next generation of professionals, I stress to them the platinum rule of healthcare service: Provide the type of care patients want given to them.

****

Learning from missed opportunities within movements like the Civil Rights Movement, I am working and promoting more opportunities for partnerships and coalitions. There is strength in numbers, and those partnerships and coalitions would have eradicated some of the various silos that hinder health care for so many people, and they would have provided more support for the change that is so desperately needed in the industry.

For example, when I took on one of my first positions at an organization in Miami at the turn of the century, I had an opportunity to execute a concept for pop-up community clinics in the most underserved zip codes. Instead, we built a stagnant 20,000 square-foot clinic. Brick-and-mortar buildings are expensive and not at all expansive or nimble enough to address the needs of the most underserved. With pop-up clinics, care would be administered in tents or leased spaces.

Looking back, I realize that I should have built a coalition around my ideas. In thinking like most of my colleagues, I had an opportunity not only to sell my ideas internally, but to build partnerships externally to make the temporary clinics a reality. Those clinics would have had a profound impact on the health of the residents of Dade County.

I learned about the dysfunctional marriage between policy/politics and health care when I was a consultant for a small boutique firm in Atlanta. The firm was tasked by the state of Georgia to create and propose a solution for greater access. My team and I presented former governor Sonny Perdue and his healthcare advisors. The concept was tantamount to that of Medicaid expansion. This was years before the Affordable Care Act was even conceived. Had I fought harder for that expansion and built coalitions surrounding the solution we devised, maybe it would have been considered in a conservative state like Georgia. I believe in piloting, and perhaps we should have started in one or two zip codes in a rural area where access is just as difficult as in an urban setting.

One of my first roles in the C-suite was as COO of a large academic medical center. I started in late summer, and the flu was extremely virulent that year. We had many patients already presenting in the emergency department with symptoms. Throughout my career, I have been adamant that the flu shot be mandatory for all healthcare professionals. Getting the flu shot is equivalent to people washing their hands before preparing or serving a meal. I did not think this would be such a radical proposition. I thought it would be embraced, particularly as we were offering it free of charge and in-house.

The pushback I received was unbelievable. There were employees who thought I was heading up an effort to take away their freedom of choice and autonomy over their bodies. I counterargued that, as employees, they were highly exposed to the flu, more so than any other people, and that we needed to be healthy in order to maintain our level of care and service. It surprises me what people hear when they are anxious, including me. Being the new guy who was forcing flu shots required me to listen to people's arguments and not merely wait to rebut.

Despite the pushback, I stood my ground, and we instituted the policy. Most hospitals and healthcare facilities require their employees to be vaccinated. Currently, we are at another crossroads surrounding the Covid vaccinations and whether they should be mandatory for healthcare professionals. I would think that most people, if not all, would want to be vaccinated, unless they have a legitimate health reason (for example, pregnancy) or a religious stipulation.

I also worked for one of the top five healthcare insurance companies in the United States, with over 400,000 employees, with a net revenue margin of about $9 billion dollars each year. During my tenure, my aim was to transition them to a healthcare company and not just an insurance company. I presented several ways we could shake up the industry and change the way people access health care in this country. True transformation in health care starts at the bedside. So, patient engagement, as well as physician accountability to improve quality, were at the top of my list through tactics such as telehealth and doctor scorecards, respectively. Like the flu shot, these ideas seem common now, but they were revolutionary then.

Unfortunately, this particular insurance company stayed well inside its silo, mainly because the silo was extremely profitable and did not engage and partner with the providers. I learned from this experience and made intentional attempts to provide platforms for partnerships with payers later in my career. It has proven to be successful from the other side of the table.

Over the years, I have had the opportunity to serve for-profit and not-for-profit boards of directors and boards of trustees for various healthcare institutions. The one commonality in healthcare governance is that there is not much African American representation. Usually, the CEO or nominating committee assembles boards without much healthcare acumen, and because of that lack of knowledge, there tends to be instances of sycophantic behavior.

Black leaders have to establish their own identity and represent African American communities within the industry. We can do, say, and have more control over those things that uniquely affect us. It will be extremely difficult for Black leaders to be progressive and pitch radical change when we are simply patterning our institutions, organizations, and methodologies after our white counterparts and conventional thinking. In doing so, we have been operating from a position of comparison instead of a position of power. The healthcare industry could have a greater impact on Black communities and progression in this country if the Black leadership feels and stays empowered.

*****

A change agent requires a fearlessness and a resolve to be unequivocal. It is definitely not for the faint of heart, but it is needed now more than ever. As Dr. Jack Cox, a good friend and colleague, once said, "If you don't like change, you're going to like irrelevance even less."

I once did a presentation where I showed a YouTube video of one person dancing in a crowd of other people. This person was dancing so animatedly that everyone else looked at him as if he was crazy.

CHAPTER FOUR

But this lone nut looked as if he was having so much fun that another person decided to ignore the crowd and dance wildly, too. The second man felt comfortable abandoning his inhibitions because he knew he was not out on the dance floor dancing wildly by himself. Before long, most of the other people joined the two men dancing and having fun.

It only takes one lone nut, or someone to follow the lone nut, to create a movement. Whether you are the initial lone nut, or the person who joins the lone nut, you are needed in health care and in this country. You are needed not just to create a moment, but to provide momentum. Either way, we need to conduct those radical, candid conversations with people to see if they are willing to join us in building a platform for change in our quest for healthy disruption.

---

[1] "Racism, Inequality, and Health Care for African Americans," by Jamila Taylor, The Century Foundation, September 2019 (tcf.org/content/report/racism-inequality-health-care-african-americans/).
[2] From "Here's What Happened When Reagan Went After Healthcare Programs. It's Not Good," by Olivia Campbell, Timeline (September 13, 2017).
[3] From "Here's What Happened When Reagan Went After Healthcare Programs. It's Not Good."
[4] From "The Reagan Administration's Budget Cuts: Their Impact on the Poor," reprint from "The Reagan Budget: A Sharp Break with the Past," *Challenger*, 24 (May–June 1981).
[5] American Hospital Association (aha.org/websites/2015-06-01-institute-diversity-health-management).
[6] "Qualities of Effective Change Agents," Michigan State University (May 28, 2019).

Chapter 5

Leadership in Unhealthy Times

"If you see something that is not right, not fair, not just, you have a moral obligation to do something about it," John Lewis, US House of Representatives, Georgia's 5th District

Much like the country, the healthcare industry is oftentimes devoid of effective leadership. Currently, our leadership lacks the talent, diversity, and compassion needed to offer quality care. It is imperative that healthcare leaders are found in unconventional spaces, where bold and up-and-coming leaders from the next generation are not only considered, but promoted. One element of disrupting our industry is replacing the privileged elite and injecting competition into a broken, structurally racist system. For real change, new leaders should be those who possess empathy and project a relatability factor.

Health care is an amalgamation of people, processes, and technology. It takes leaders with the temerity and desire to want to change, but also people who are willing to continue to bring their whole selves to sordid conditions, even when those in power are pushing the change agents to reform. The platinum rule must stay steady in one's psyche and let it be the guide.

I am passionate about finding, teaching, mentoring, and training those leaders who are willing to shake things up. However, they must be willing to work, put in the time, and withstand the pressure and resistance they are sure to encounter.

*****

I read and study biographies of great leaders from the past. I admire Black leaders, in particular, given what they have had to overcome. They crossed through the fires of racism, segregation, discrimination, oppression, and injustices. I have thoroughly examined the lives of writers, activists, entrepreneurs, and other historical figures who have inspired me to develop strong leadership qualities and make it their mission to bring others along with them on the journey.

I read the book *Why Should White Guys Have All the Fun?* an autobiographical account written by Black business mogul Reginald Lewis. The book transformed my thinking of what is possible. This subsequently led me to research other Black entrepreneurs, from Madam C. J. Walker to current trailblazers such as philanthropist Robert Smith.

Recently, I was impressed by Smith, who was the commencement speaker at Morehouse College in 2018. During his speech, he announced that he was donating over $40 million to pay off the school debt for the Class of 2018. I was impressed by Smith's largess but, more important, by the audacity behind it. It is one thing to make a gift, but it is another to follow that gift with inspiration and meaning. I am sure that after Smith made that gift, everyone in the audience was asking, "What exactly is private equity?" and

CHAPTER FIVE

"How can I break into it?" That is influence, not a gift, not being ostentatious, but opening hearts and minds to possibilities.

Because of history, and in the spirit of *Sankofa*, the study and storytelling aspect of Black trials and triumphs is not new. It is ancestral dating back to roots in Africa to slavery to the Civil Rights Movement to today's protest after the murder of George Floyd. Even the intentional disconnect and purposeful prevention working to keep Black people from our history, families, homeland, education, health, and overall wealth through structural racism has not curbed progress, no matter how incremental. Black people are resilient, and it is one of our greatest superpowers. Black people glean perspective and process information when our lineage is detailed.

Unfortunately, Black people's struggle and determination to make a way, even when a vision for the future may look bleak, pits Black leaders against one another. This is purposeful as well. Because Black health and wealth have yet to be realized, Black leaders often examine in great detail how to improve our position in this country. The privileged would have you believe that there is only one pathway to success. When Black people espouse their views and it is contradictory to others or is not the popular perspective, they are vilified or they denounce one another. This weakens Black people's station even further in this country and weakens our superpower to fight for equity, which will ultimately lead to equality and wealth.

As the country goes, so too goes health care in America. There have been countless times when I have seen this ruinous trend unfold among Black leaders in health care.

Booker T. Washington was committed to the idea of community and cooperative economics and believed that people could succeed if they "pulled themselves up by their bootstraps." Popular among

HEALTHY DISRUPTION

some white elites, this sentiment was invoked by many Black people who were provided an opportunity to work for and purchase an asset that would appreciate (for example, land). This is a firm philosophy if you have an actual boot in the first place. Because structural racism is so pervasive, the playing field is not always level. However, I admire Washington's leadership in education as a former slave and as a voice for the newly minted and upwardly mobile Black middle class, many of whom were former slaves. Washington reminds me a lot of my grandfather's mentality as a sharecropper in Mississippi.

Conversely, I have read WEB DuBois's book *The Souls of Black Folk* many times. It is a literary work that displays DuBois's expertise as a sociologist and his experiences as a Black man in America. There is a duality of existence for many Black Americans: having to project one character for a class of people and then another that is more authentic. This holds true for Black people in leadership, particularly those in health care.

Consequently, DuBois's belief that The Talented Tenth would uplift the entire race, a philosophy that he later clarified and retracted shortly before his death, is contrarian to my belief that you are only as good as your opportunities and the exposure to them. While I respect DuBois's commitment to education and Black leadership in our communities, the requirements to be part of the Talented Tenth would probably be out of reach for many of us, including me. The only reason I am where I am is because of the opportunities afforded to me. People saw potential even if it was unrealized. Good leaders can come from almost anywhere and is not just reserved for the elite few.

I respect and honor the legacy of the Reverend Dr. Martin Luther King Jr. As a child, I listened as my mother played his speeches over and over. I memorized most of them by the time I was in middle school. Thus, I possessed a rather extensive vocabulary for a 12-year-old because I used many of the words and phrases from King's speeches.

One of the reasons I attended Morehouse was because Dr. King was a graduate 50 years before I was. He was eloquent in his sermons, speeches, and writings, but he was not just spouting soaring words and platitudes of peace. He spoke out on war, poverty, and international injustices and encouraged a generation to address them nonviolently. King was an effective leader who formed coalitions of black and white, Catholic and Protestant, rich and poor, and Northern and Southern.

King was not considered dangerous until he denounced two major issues in America: the war in Vietnam and the treatment of poor people in this country. Ironically, war is rampant in America (the United States just ended the war in Afghanistan after 20 years but still occupies countries abroad) and the working poor have never been more prevalent, particularly as the pandemic rages onward. Most people think that King was moderate, but he was quite radical, especially toward the end of his life.

The public, namely by way of the privileged, have worked to draw distinctions between King and Malcolm X. However, much like Washington and DuBois, King and Malcolm X were more similar than different, especially as each leader became more enlightened and aware of the systemic forces in the United States. For as long as I can remember, I looked to Malcolm for inspiration, self-actualization, and transformation. I read *The Autobiography of Malcolm X* when I was 11, and to this day, I consider it one of my favorite books. Malcolm changed the conversation on racism and injustice and made us look at gaining equality from alternative angles.

HEALTHY DISRUPTION

I have also studied the writings and speeches of James Baldwin, another radical Black leader who had a clear and tangible message. There is so much pain, strength, and struggle in his writings that his message resonates with me and my life experiences.

Radicalism requires three key aspects in leadership: engagement, courage, and sacrifice. If you take a more modern-day example of the temerity—or the lack thereof—to revolutionize hearts and minds, you can pull Michael Jordan's trajectory to fame and success in the 1980's. Jordan is one of the most gifted and talented basketball players that I have ever had the pleasure of witnessing play ball. No one compares to his uncanny desire and pursuit to win games. However, like King, I continuously wonder what certain Black leaders have done to make their teams, race, or community better.

Jordan thrilled us with his basketball abilities and his various styles of sneakers, but I am not sure that Black leaders, especially those with a platform, have the luxury of being agnostic. The attitude that "Republicans wear sneakers, too" will not work in modern times, particularly for Black leaders. Jordan recently donated $100 million dollars over a period of ten years to causes for Black equality. Leaders cannot wait to be great. In other words, anyone can jump on the bandwagon and donate to a cause after it is cool to do so or everyone has already called out the injustices.

In his book *Forty Million Dollar Slaves: The Rise, Fall, and Redemption of the Black Athlete*, William Rhoden wrote, "Leaders have to possess a certain inner ability to stick their necks out and sometimes get it chopped by way of a lost endorsement and even being 'black' balled from your own league at the top of your game."[1] From this perspective, Colin Kaepernick comes to mind.

CHAPTER FIVE

Unfortunately, we have a disproportionate number of leaders in health care who are much like Jordan. They are highly gifted, charismatic, and "look the part" but do not demonstrate those three basic characteristics of engagement, courage, and sacrifice. Many Black leaders are not willing to engage in the community, make the team around them better (mentor, provide opportunities for the next generation), nor sacrifice by placing a cause or an issue above their own agenda or success to call out injustices. Consequently, the greatest individual athlete of all time, in my opinion, was Muhammad Ali. This man, beyond reproach, was committed to all three, and we see the impact that it ultimately had on American society.

These are the leaders who came before us, those whose message still speaks long after they have departed the planet. I reflect on their words, writings, and teachings as a compass as I develop those leaderships qualities that make me most effective. It is this type of courage, honor, discipline, and radicalism that is needed not only for health care to change, but for the country to change, too.

*****

As the pandemic continues to intensify, another deficit that is painfully obvious is the industry's lack of talent. This is one of the most glaring sins of omission we routinely commit. There is a dearth of representation of people of color and women in leadership, administrative, and care delivery spaces. It is puzzling that more minorities are not elevated within the healthcare ranks as we care for people who look more like us. Many communities find it difficult to trust outsiders. Having healthcare providers of color who could go into communities, gain trust, and provide quality care would be essential for success during the pandemic.

HEALTHY DISRUPTION

The healthcare industry is one of the most isolated, siloed industries. We promote from within, with narrow definitions of what qualifies as the right expertise. We retreat to standards that are comfortable for the privileged rather than welcoming those from other fields or those with different professional experiences. We are incredibly insular, without accountability from other industries, hence the ballooning of health care as a percentage of the GDP. We are stuck in a cycle of repeating initiatives and methods that do not work.

It is said that Albert Einstein defined *insanity* as doing the same thing over and over but expecting different results, which accurately describes the healthcare industry. Instead of wasting time trying to revive the same tired methods, effective leaders should seek solutions around the seven C's:

- **Culture.** As Peter Drucker once stated, culture trumps strategy. Often, leaders start off wrong because they are not addressing the culture that houses the people who are responsible for the success or failure of the organization.
- **Consolidation.** Health care is continuously consolidating under the tent of big corporations and health systems. We should ask, "How are those newly formed organizations leveraging their size to improve community health and not just administer health care?"
- **Commercialization.** The reason the investment side of health care is skyrocketing is due to the productization of health care. All healthcare leaders and organizations should be thinking of productization, product differentiation, and packaging and marketing of products.
- **Consumerism.** Americans value convenience, retail health care is all the rage. Drug stores and supermarkets are

CHAPTER FIVE

working hard to become a one-stop shop healthcare provider. These retailers are providing pharmacies and clinics staffed by nurse practitioners and offering exams, consultations, medicine, and vaccinations, alongside food and other necessities most people shop for. The healthcare leader's challenge is figuring out how the one-stop approach helps communities of color.

- **Coalition-building.** Partnerships are occurring less frequently given consolidation and all the merger and acquisition activity over recent years. Partnerships, whether formal or informal, should be occurring much more frequently in health care. Moreover, healthcare institutions should be partnering with organizations outside health care to demonstrate differentiation, offer a suite of services (not just administer care), and work to bring more options to patients.
- **Concept-to-execution.** Just as in any other industry, healthcare leaders should also not have pie-in-the-sky, pipe dreams, but they should focus on what and who can execute the top two or three things in a specified time frame.
- **Control.** Control is perceived, given, taken, or vapor in health care. Unfortunately, it is often not earned. The implicit hierarchies in health care have been in place for hundreds of years. Be honest with yourself, your team, and your colleagues about the control you have.

These identification and relatability factors are the cornerstone of a leader's superpower, particularly in the healthcare industry, which is the perfect amalgamation of people, processes, and technology. Consequently, there are many traps and pitfalls of leadership. As the saying goes, "Heavy is the head that wears the crown." This is especially true for Black leaders in the industry for several reasons.

- Typically, we are not well-represented, and we occupy positions with no real authority or decision-making power.
- The status quo benefits those who are ensconced in this antiquated industry. They are better able to leverage their positions for more control and more money.
- Although most corporations claim to champion diversity, equity, and inclusion, the reality on the ground is quite different. The empty DEI efforts, affinity and employee groups, and newly developed "belonging" as part of addressing diversity is often inauthentic. It usually hearkens back to culture and what and who the organization really is.

The industry has a few dirty little secrets that we should all be aware of. It is the behind-the-scenes knowledge that keeps health care from being accessible to marginalized communities. So, it is imperative that we highlight these long-lasting issues in health care to bring awareness and address the problems.

Unfortunately, there is very little authenticity around diversity, equity, and inclusion in the industry. Many corporations merely pay lip service to these values, while their actions lack substance, capital, and skill set to recruit, retain, and promote effective leaders of color. Black leaders who dare to speak up are implicitly or explicitly silenced or ignored. Their effectiveness is muted. There is no incentive for them to stay where they are not wanted, and the industry is poorer for it. Even the hiring of a chief diversity and inclusion officer with no real authority or team is shameful

CHAPTER FIVE

and demonstrates a company's true commitment to real DEI transformation.

The hierarchy is so stark, no matter how qualified you are, it is difficult to make it to authentic positions of power. Those rarefied positions are reserved for the privileged few. As in any industry, those who want to rise through the ranks must pay their dues, but those dues are financially and politically expensive.

Volume and reimbursement is king. Value-based care is defined in so many different ways to so many different people, which is why it is so elusive. Unfortunately, about 90 percent of health care is still playing the fee-for-service game, including the providers, payers, pharmaceutical companies, and patients. While conducting a service and then expecting to get paid for it is an American trait, it should not be how health care is administered. I doubt anyone wants to be in the hospital, yet hospitals are usually paid by how many bodies are in beds throughout their facility.

Reimbursement still drives most decisions from providers and payers. Unfortunately, hospitals in communities of color are not reimbursed at the same rates as hospitals in the suburbs because they have poorer populations who are using Medicaid. The payer mix deters payers from negotiating higher rates for those who need care the most.

Hospitals are the center of the healthcare universe and should not be. When patients are most vulnerable, sick, and weary, the healthcare industry asks them to go to a place full of other sick and weary people. This has been the norm for centuries in this country. Hospitals are expensive and can be the largest drain on the American healthcare system.

HEALTHY DISRUPTION

The healthcare industry is lazy but lucrative. For years, the industry has approached care delivery as a one-size-fits-all model. This has been especially true since managed care and population health were newly introduced as tactics to mitigate rising healthcare costs. Costs have risen year over year in health care since the 1970s. It only slowed when the ACA was signed. Healthcare leadership seems to be concerned less with innovations that would allow us to customize care for patients, focus on one zip code for the overall health of that specific community, incorporate the social determinants of health, and partner with organizations that can help improve health and not just health care.

The healthcare industry is not as altruistic as it claims. Because health care was born out of church-based institutions and Christian denominations (Catholic, Lutheran, Methodist, and Baptist), the guiding principles were rooted in the tenets of Christ. This allowed for tax exemptions and sizable gifts to and from foundations. Even not-for-profit institutions are absolutely about the profit. They must demonstrate value through finances.

Health care is a business, one of the biggest businesses in America by GDP standards. Since its inception, the industry has claimed to be guided by Christianity. However, the bottom line is always front of mind for healthcare leaders. The new-aged, free-thinking healthcare leader will need to take these dirty little secrets, apply the seven C's, and work to execute on strategy. To transform the industry, nimbleness in decision-making and a relatable leadership style is required. Relatability emanates from vulnerability. This was never truer and more needed than during the pandemic. A relatable leader can execute with humanely and effectively. The same holds true for transformation in America as well.

CHAPTER FIVE

Leaders in the healthcare industry must hold a burning desire for change and a tough stomach. Once developed, that tough stomach will be tested at times and become nauseous with a pit of uneasiness that dominates their thoughts. Within an insular, bureaucratic, hierarchical system like health care, leaders will be told they are crazy; their ideas will not work; "We've always done it this way, and we're not changing"; or there are not enough resources to do what they want done.

It is extremely difficult. The industry has fossilized, and working to break into the upper echelon of the privileged leadership circle for control is daunting. The gatekeepers have been charged to keep out people who look like me, which makes change from within almost impossible. Then again, the status quo that they guard so closely has padded many pockets, purchased many second houses, and led to cushy retirement packages for the privileged.

The resistance and pushback has certainly worn me down, but it has also served as fuel and a reminder that I am on the right track. If the more enlightened leaders are willing to listen, respect differences, and allow reform to take place, resistance can create a healthy tension. It can generate dialogue, and serve as a catalyst for more conversation and understanding.

Not to be confused, but I am extremely complicit in where and what health care has become: slow, complacent, not diverse enough, exclusionary, elitist. Perhaps, I am more like Jordan (definitely not by way of basketball) than I think. Perhaps, I have shown a level of conceit and self-worth and demonstrated apathy when empathy and action were required. Even in kindergarten, I tended to color outside the lines. That probably explains the positions I have taken, decisions I have rendered, partnerships I have established, and investments I have made.

HEALTHY DISRUPTION

So, as a leader, I am willing to abandon the norms and engage in revolutionary and evolutionary thinking to get things done. I am not intimidated by the good old boys' network or the circle of a privileged few in our industry, but sometimes I need to look internally and externally for inspiration.

I often think about my daughter and the leadership scarcity that she has seen throughout her short life. She was born during the Obama Administration and endured a troubling season during the Trump Administration. She has only known two presidents in her life, and they could not be more different. Subsequently, she has witnessed disturbing events such as war, protests, and viewpoints that have led to unrest and injustices. I worry that the absence of leadership will shape her and that she will not have the same heroes that I did during my childhood. And then I slap myself back to reality. I remind myself that it starts with me, and I need to become the best leader I can for her and my entire family.

As leaders from eras past have shown us, when you walk through the fire, you have something important to say. The messaging must resonate with the people we are committed to serve and lead. Be the type of leader who can use your experiences to make you better, more flexible, more compassionate, more empathetic, and much more action-oriented.

****

Healthcare leaders have the power to serve as a catalyst for change. We can restore hope and mobilize for a better future. Although the healthcare industry has many flaws and has made many stumbles along the way, it is not all gloom and doom. WEB DuBois said, "Believe in Life! Always human beings will live and progress to a greater, broader, and fuller life."

CHAPTER FIVE

Like America, health care has made inroads to create structural and sustained change. I have detected a rising shared consciousness, especially in the younger generations. They operate with a growth mindset and do not mind challenging the status quo, not only in the healthcare industry, but in political and socioeconomic arenas. Those who are coming along behind me have an ability to mobilize in the wake of the social injustices they see in our society, and I predict that the next arena they disrupt will be health care.

From an African American perspective, there is also hope. I am excited to see incremental changes in the industry, especially for Black leaders. There are black-owned companies that I have invested in that are remaining true to the communities they serve. They are addressing some of the most pressing issues in health care, such as chronic disease management, disjointed continuum of care, and the digital divide.

Black leaders in health care have an opportunity and a pivotal responsibility to seize this moment, create momentum, and start a movement to fundamentally change the industry. Because of the anguish, anxiety, and injustices that we have lived through, Black people are uniquely equipped and qualified for this moment. As my Spelman sister Stacey Abrams wrote, "Our time is now." I would hate to see us squander it.

---

[1]*Forty Million Dollar Slaves: The Rise, Fall, and Redemption of the Black Athlete*, by William C. Rhoden (Crown, 2007).

Chapter 6

Finding the Way Forward to a Healthy Future

"I am no longer accepting the things I cannot change; I am changing the things I cannot accept." Dr. Angela Davis

I watched the movie *The Color Purple* for the first time with my parents when I was eight or nine years old. The movie's most cathartic point is toward the end, culminating with the song "Maybe God Is Tryin' to Tell You Something." This song reverberates in my head to this day when confronted with a decision, an unruly person, an injustice, or any impediment to my progress.

I am convinced that the events of 2020 and 2021 were not by happenstance. The confluence of the three P's (pandemic, protests, and profit) in our world, our country, and our professions is, in fact, God trying to tell us something. We would be doing our country and the healthcare industry a disservice if we did not thoroughly examine the events before us and work together for meaningful change. This audit cannot come by way of a checklist or a surface-level analysis so that those who are privileged can maintain their positions and current lifestyles.

HEALTHY DISRUPTION

My grandfather would rant about the need to always be thorough, that is to say, "Inspect what you expect." Black people will not materially change their station in this country nor in health care until we thoroughly investigate those who have attained their position today and subsequently construct structural barriers that avert our advancement.

One of Dr. King's most profound books was entitled *Where Do We Go From Here? Chaos or Community?* I would contend that where the country and the industry stand currently, it is probably both. King analyzed race relations, communities, and war—issues that continue to plague this country today. As Black leaders, our work is never complete, and it is our responsibility to keep the work going, even when some of us may not see the need to do so. This reality makes many Black leaders anxious, but it is necessary if we are ever going to realize equality in this country.

While catastrophic and extremely painful, I believe the three P's and the events that ensued in 2020 were necessary. Chaos is what sets disruption in motion. Though the events that sparked them were tragic, we needed the chaos to erupt in such a way that we could no longer ignore it. It cannot be a futile roundtable with a few Black people talking about diversity under the auspices of a "DEI movement."

This chaos should manifest into radical candor in our discussions, relationships, organizations, partnerships, and professions. If we do not take advantage of the chaos, we risk squandering the resulting momentum. We must engage and involve the community. Chaos should serve a specific purpose, a means to an end. It should serve as a spark to set movements in motion. Once we have fought and disrupted the systems that have been in place for generations, we

CHAPTER SIX

need a collective place to go. Our communities should provide that place. Unfortunately, communities of color are not sustainable. They are rife with unemployment, crime, food insecurities, inadequate housing, substandard schools, and other determinants that keep us unhealthy. Healthy disruption occurs when temporary chaos leads to the candor we crave, while simultaneously sparking the needed attention and rebuilding of disenfranchised communities.

Black people are some of the most spiritual, soulful, dedicated, hard-working, and communal people on the planet. I am definitely not knocking any other race, but I am working to uplift my own. The amalgamation of these unique innate attributes should be used now more than ever to create a better, stronger, healthier, and unified country and industry.

*****

Health care is everybody's business. It is the business of every corporation, foundation, and human being on the planet because it is so interconnected to everything we do. You can measure the wealth of any country by examining and understanding its approach to health.

> "Moving forward is one of the most important decisions we can make in life, because it allows us to grow, learn new lessons, . . . and overcome our adversities." Dr. Peter Nieman, *Moving Forward*

In finding a way forward, leaders should establish goals that will propel us in a direction that is conducive and relevant for an expedient evolution to occur. My indiscriminate passion for justice drew me into the healthcare industry, and it motivates me every day to

HEALTHY DISRUPTION

work for a better system and for a better country. How we get there is less important than that we get there at all.

As previously presented, the seven C's occurring in health care are unfolding rapidly. The five P's are siloed and should be further integrated as quickly as possible. As such, community health down to the zip code must be enforced because the dirty little secrets of health care prevail. There should be goals established and executed against these thoughts while patterning the successes and pitfalls of leaders of the past and leveraging respective backgrounds to bring diversity of thought to the process.

However, setting goals and working to set strategies against those goals can be tricky, if not elusive if there is disagreement and misalignment on the issues, priorities, and capital needed. If not undertaken with care, we can become disjointed because there is a lack of harmony among us. This is often an intentional tactic of the privileged to divide Black leadership and limit our strides. It is important that Black leaders establish a framework that will focus and guide our efforts and serve as a recalibration if we veer off course.

Most people in business and beyond are familiar and subscribe to SMART (**S**pecific, **M**easurable, **A**chievable or **A**mbitious, **R**ealistic or **R**elevant, and **T**imebound) objectives for the assertion on goal-setting. I think there are two pertinent points germane to anyone who is working to transform this country and the healthcare industry: (1) It is important to add "**M**indset of growth" to the "**M**," and (2) over the last few years, companies have added "**I**nclusion" and "**E**quity" to the SMART formula because "inclusion and equity do not happen by accident and it can be measured in a timebound manner."

CHAPTER SIX

Some companies have applied the SMARTIE method and made their boards responsible for more inclusion and equity. SMARTIE goals "embrace power with others. When people and communities, particularly those impacted by a goal, are included in a way that shares power, the process shrinks disparities and leads to more equitable outcomes."[1]

Black people have the prowess to promote and proliferate objectives to obtain this type of power and equitable outcomes if we embrace the seven C's within the five P's. The following suggestions are also important to stimulate healthy solutions:

- **Focus on health equity, not necessarily equality.** Equality is the vision; equity is the goal. Equity, as previously portrayed, is synonymous with ownership, stake, and control of an entity, venture, or company. Over time, equity will ultimately lead to more power, which will ultimately lead to equality. Equality has been so elusive, dating back to slavery, Jim Crow, and the Civil Rights Movement, and due to the structures that are cemented into the American psyche. However, that psyche weakens with control.

- **Create concepts for community health to thrive.** An outreach to a specific community from any company, person, or venture should be the norm in this country. Further, there should be provisions and tax breaks for companies that can demonstrate dedication and positive change in defined zip codes. These approaches should be anchored in data and technology. Ventures such as telehealth and home health should serve as guideposts for additional ventures along the way, with the goal of getting to more personalized, customized care and deep considerations for the social determinants of health for patients.

- **Proliferate the platform of the ACA.** Passed in 2010, states have a lot of control over the direction of the ACA. It has withstood over 40 appeals to date, all the way up to the Supreme Court. Now entrenched in US law and policy, states have the autonomy to raise the federal poverty line qualifications for Medicaid as an element of the ACA. The ACA could embed value-based care tactics and tools into the care delivery system; expand the usage of health savings accounts (HSAs), which would help most families dealing with chronic diseases; and allow the essential and frontline work ("working poor") to qualify for more health benefits at a cheaper insurance rate. While not perfect, the ACA's platform is established and should be leveraged to break the employer-sponsored healthcare system and enable more consumer-driven care.
- **Find a common thread and alignment in solutions across the sectors of health care.** The healthcare industry can, and sometimes does, have the best intentions. However, those intentions are derailed because there is not much incentive alignment among the five P's within health care. There have been outfits to solely work on this issue and this issue alone before tackling others. At times, that is valiant, as the most difficult obstacle to overcome is which P out of the five is going to bear the most risk, responsibility, and reward.
- **Develop partnerships that span the spectrum to increase engagement and mitigate risk.** Comfort is analogous to

complacency. It is easy to stay siloed and insular because it supports the status quo. Primarily, the privileged revert to the insular type of thinking or "solutions" when other ideas seem too difficult or fail on the first try. However, partnerships outside of health care within governmental agencies, private institutions, and various corporations should not only be explored but be executed expeditiously. Partnerships have the power to address disparities within the social determinants of health, create incentives for alignment, and decouple risk within health care. However, these actions require a growth mindset and tangible milestones for partnerships to flourish.

- **Engage foundations, billionaires, and some private equity with statistics and outcomes.** There continues to be an influx of capital into health care. During the last quarter of 2020, there was over $41 billion that was invested into the healthcare space. However, many companies and ventures of color still struggle to find funding for their ideas. Private equity and venture capital is certainly a proven route to garner an investment, but also connect with foundations, holding companies, and other corporations that have venture arms for specific products. Many private equity companies are beholden to their investors to make an exit with certain companies. Conversely, other avenues such as foundations and holding companies can invest, aid in operations, and not have the same pressures to find an exit for ROI 3x of the initial investment. In addition, many health systems are starting venture arms, and a plethora of Fortune 500 companies already have an established fund for investing. Billionaires, especially those who are established and have demonstrated generational wealth over time, should have an obligation to invest in communities of color and other related interests. I am against additional taxation, even for those making ten figures or more. Billionaires and their estates have gotten so astute at tax loopholes, there is no point to offering additional ones. However, there should be some requirement from a healthcare perspective where a billionaire has to engage. Given that health care is everyone's business, and that America will be stronger once health care is improved in this country, it should be a requirement for the top two to three percent of earners.

- **Mold the talent pipeline of the future to challenge the status quo.** Mentor. Teach. Invest. The next generation of leaders cannot adopt the same stale, tired mentality that has been invoked by the privileged for centuries. Leaders, especially Black leaders, must mentor through methods that promote entrepreneurship, intrapreneurship, equity, and disruption. Leaders, corporations, companies, and foundations should look to invest (not just with funds, but other methods as well) in HBCUs. It is imperative that our youth think and develop their own ideas and concepts. Leaders should be willing to hire people who demonstrate potential, but may not have as much experience. Management consultant Peter Drucker stated, "The only way to teach responsibility is to give it." Innovation, which is sorely needed in this country and in health care, emanates from the younger generation.

CHAPTER SIX

Whether personal or professional, an individual or a corporation, small or large , Black or white, SMARTIE goals can and should be applied to produce the most advantageous outcomes for all. Let the platinum rule of humanity be the guide, and let the need to improve overall community health be the goal.

For instance, financiers are beginning to realize the power, potential outcomes, and return on investment (ROI) surrounding social impact funds. The realization comes by way of a common practice in venture capital and private equity of going deep into the business to understand opportunities and barriers while exploiting potential growth opportunities. Within social impact funds, this deep dive usually occurs in impoverished, disadvantaged communities. In this instance, these communities can benefit from these ventures.

Obviously, starting, sustaining, and achieving success with any of these suggestions requires capital. As stated, there is an abundance of private equity money afoot in health care. To ensure that prudence is the primary practice of spending and investing money against established goals and ventures, leaders can:

- Pool money and resources with colleagues, friends, and trusted family members. Then invest in companies and ventures that are aligned with the goals you set.
- Start a fund specific to one of the causes you are championing, and socialize to raise capital.
- Research existing investing vehicles (private equity, special purpose acquisition company [SPAC], social impact fund), and begin part of the group through a modest investment.
- Invest in ventures that will disrupt the status quo, and operate with a partnership mentality to address all social

determinants of health for employees and for marginalized communities.
- Donate a portion of the dividends to social causes and organizations doing the work in their communities.
- Ensure that a portion of the dividends are paid back to a disenfranchised community or a group that is being affected.
- Set pay-out contingencies based on outcomes individually based or within the community that is being impacted.

When large employers, individual leaders, and financiers partner with one another to break through the ineffective standardization of the past, we can move toward a more personalized system of care that lets people pursue health and access care in ways that work for them.

*****

Currently, the money is in the medicine, not the cure, but that needs to change. The healthcare system should be incentivized to reward positive outcomes for patients. As a country and as a society, we should be fervently advocating, promoting, and executing these outcomes because they would be effective ways to disrupt the healthcare system.

My suggestions for a better future in health care can create massive inroads, new partnerships, and even unfound wealth to many people and new ventures. However, my suggestions are incremental and serve as a stopgap for the current malaise we are enduring in this industry and throughout this country.

A vision for a better future in health care must be as audacious as it has ever been tantamount to the moment that God has put before us.

CHAPTER SIX

After pondering ways forward with a preponderance of data, the vision for a better, more sustained, and equitable healthcare system and even country is twofold:

- Migrate to a single-payer system, and achieve universal health care for all.
- Give reparations to Black people in the United States.

Many would say that the ACA is and was the precursor to universal health care. However, the SSA signed by President Franklin Roosevelt, as well as the Medicare program introduced by President Lyndon Johnson, were launching pads for a single-payer system. In the meantime, the law makes sure that most of the uninsured population had the ability to gain access to insurance and coverage. The ACA also brought awareness to the fact that everyone needs insurance but does not have access because they are unemployed or underemployed and do not receive insurance benefits.

Universal health care would eventually ameliorate all the issues that continue to be present in the industry, such as risk, value-based care, for example. The reason these concepts have never been fully implemented is because the incentives of the five P's has been misaligned for generations. A single-payer system would, ultimately, solve for this major hurdle in health care.

This may be somewhat of a controversial stand, particularly for a healthcare executive who has worked in three of the five P's and has been a patient. However, I am a firm believer that universal health care could be the healthier disrupter lever yet. I have yet to commit to Medicare for all being the solution. In fact, I am not certain that the government should actually be the primary operator of a universal healthcare insurance platform. The difference, albeit a bit

HEALTHY DISRUPTION

nuanced, is that there would be a significant investment to the government to solve for gaps in infrastructure to insure all Americans.

I like the freedom of choice that the ACA offers as part of the exchange and that the payer could be part of and even improve upon the exchange. Moreover, the payer could also build and promote products within Medicare Advantage, Medicaid, and the exchanges. Meanwhile, payers and pharmaceutical companies could continue to enhance care delivery, essentially only focused on quality of care under one payer construct and evaluation methodology.

With the eradication of contracts based on percentages of Medicare, new care delivery models and outfits could flourish without the pressures of reimbursement and offer care under the single-payer guidelines. This would lower healthcare costs, increase access, and provide satisfaction as the industry adheres to real-time data and leverages technology under the new model.

Regarding reparations, Black people built this country and deserve to be compensated. Further arguments to support reparations include the structural and systemic racist policies, systems, and mentalities that still exist that inhibit Black people from our full potential, compounded by more than 400 years of slavery and consistent oppression thereafter. I am working to teach my daughter that she has a right to everything but is not entitled to anything. Reparations, for me, is not about entitlement; it is about a level playing field.

One of the reasons I am such a vocal evangelist for reparations is because many African Americans will be hard-pressed to overcome systemic and structural racist policies and mentalities without the opportunities to create and establish equity. When most people think of reparations, they think of a large cash payout to ancestors of African slaves, but reparations can also come in many forms.

CHAPTER SIX

Reparations could even be prescribed by way of health, not necessarily health care. Anything that impacts one's health—for example, the social determinants of health—could be an avenue to be explored as part of a reparations package for Black people. Affirmative action, like the ACA, scratched the surface on disruption. This country should be in full support of finally knocking down barriers to full and healthy disruption and seriously discuss, design, and implement reparations for Black people in the United States.

*****

After 25 years in health care, I have seen a lot, and I have learned a lot. Some days, I am discouraged and want to give up, but I cannot ignore that glimmer of hope on the horizon. I have heard it said that you can go three weeks without food and three days without water, but you cannot go three hours without hope. So, I cling to hope because that is what moves me forward. I am going to use the tools I have and the resources that are before me to make a difference.

The global events of 2020 turned this world upside down. Because of that, we are a changed people, a changed country. But I hope we not only learned the lessons of the past year, but that we are applying them so that we have access, equity, inclusion, and diversity for everyone in the healthcare system and in our country.

This is where I apply the spirit of *Sankofa* and the acronym I AM (information, access, and money). If we can make sure everyone has these, we could go a long way in empowering, educating, edifying, and providing equity for everyone. This is important in making the healthcare industry better because an empowered patient is an informed one.

Chaos and confrontation are needed for change to our communities and position in this country. Finding equity is the initial step

HEALTHY DISRUPTION

to that fiscal process of equality. I doubt that anything is going to be given to us, nor are the injustices that have been the prevailing philosophy of this country going to be rectified. However, Black people are now at an extraordinarily unique position with all that has occurred over the course of this past year, and we are perfectly poised to take control of our own future.

Personally, this past year has been a struggle. I have seen how intricate and indispensable health is to a specific group of people. In every fiber of my being, I know that a person's health is inextricably tied to his or her ability to create and maintain wealth. While equity is the first step to financial freedom, Black peoples' health must be the precursor to everything. Health begins where Africans began. Black people must reclaim the spirit of *Sankofa*, the mentality of *Ubuntu*, and develop and keep the growth mindset. Healthy disruption begins with our mental health and state. Disruption comes by way of leveraging forces around us for the greater good.

"Collectively, we have an opportunity to create a better world, where possibilities are endless and reflect the best of who we are as humans."[2]

---

[1] "Be a Smartie: An Equity-Forward Approach to Goal Setting," Giving USA (February 8, 2021).
[2] "Be a Smartie: An Equity-Forward Approach to Goal Setting."

Epilogue

The Healthy Connection Between Compassion, Empathy, and Disruption

"One city, one country, one state . . . some place to be nobody . . . some place you wouldn't know probably." Nas

Every American should have the basic right to health and health care, and they should have access to the resources that would help them to improve their quality of life free from inhibition or regardless of their current station in society. This basic right is fundamental to amassing wealth in this country and has been denied to many Black people for generations.

Given this tender time in our nation, we have a unique opportunity to usher in new terms, policies, standards, and laws predicated on America's original premise: life, liberty, and the pursuit of happiness. To abolish the hypocrisy of the Declaration of Independence, our country needs to conduct authentic, candid confrontations—not

HEALTHY DISRUPTION

just conversations among the privileged and those who have been disenfranchised for years.

For the first time that I can remember, Black people and the privileged now can find common ground. Both groups feel separated from government and share a loss of control. We have seen this sentiment manifested over the last year through the protests after the murder of George Floyd to the riot on the nation's Capital building. The difference is that Black people have never had control, but for centuries, white people and the privileged have had inroads to power through systemic forces in this country.

I have referenced the privileged throughout this book. I would wager that many of them have placed their own definitions on the meaning of *privileged*; dismissed my definition of *privileged* as coming from my personal bias, and they are confused by the fact that my anger is not aimed at any particular reader; or they rejected the entire thesis that there is a privileged structure in America that systemically oppresses the disenfranchised, consciously or subconsciously.
I would contend that all three possibilities are catastrophically myopic and serve as the catalyst for many of the sustaining issues in this country. Privilege is a mindset and must constantly be studied and course-corrected to affect change.

America is privileged and is a byproduct of capitalism, which led to the need, greed, and ills of slavery. I believe in free trade and free markets, but not at the expense of other human beings. The privileged must not just forgo their privilege; they must recognize, acknowledge, and transform their privilege in order to confront the disparities that are continuing to intensify acutely as we experience the three P's (pandemic, protests, and profit) in this country.

EPILOGUE

Privilege is defined as "an advantage or immunity available only to a particular person or group and the ability to express the advantage without repercussion or persecution." Certain words and phrases from this definition stand out to me: *advantage, immunity, available,* and *without repercussion.* Like growth, privilege starts and ends as a mindset.

America is full of privileged people—me included. All of us are predisposed to certain insights that others are not, but we must examine where our respective privileges may become prejudicial and structural and prohibit other human beings from advancing. However, the dichotomy among those who are privileged and the treatment of Black people in this country is glaring, tangible, and obvious, and these instances are referenced throughout this book.

If these illustrations are not easily discernible to you, then the privileged class described in this text likely depicts you, and you are probably an unknowing accomplice. Worse yet, you may be a person who advocates privileged thinking and structural racism. Moreover, you are not exempt from privilege simply because you are not white.

> **"You can't lead the people if you don't love the people. You can't save the people if you don't serve the people." Cornel West**

All privileged people are not white. Most are Caucasian, given the predominance of their race in America; but in my career, I have encountered the privileged mindset in all ethnicities and genders. In fact, when people of other ethnicities do not see and acknowledge their privilege, it is often more dangerous because it disrupts the collective

HEALTHY DISRUPTION

consciousness and destroys any ability for coalition-building. They often protect their privilege even more vigorously than whites. However, we have all been oppressed by the system, and instead of protecting our privilege and becoming an entrenched elitist class, we need to channel that oppression into change.

The healthcare industry, like this country, has a unique opportunity. Because of its mission, whether authentic or misguided, people's health and their access to a quality life is the most basic and fundamental right. We can seize this opportunity by looking within ourselves and our country to disrupt the current corrupt healthcare system. It is the first and only right that will equalize the privileged and the disenfranchised and ultimately lead to a narrowing of the wealth gap. The elementary postulate of health care is embedded in humanity. Health care should lead with humanity, and this is humanity in action.

> "One love."
>
> Robert (Bob) Nesta Marley

When examining humanity, Thomas Hobbes, author of *Leviathan*, wrote, "A [person's] conscience and judgement is the same thing; and as judgement, so also the conscience, may be erroneous."[1] Hobbes, a steadfast detractor of morality and an eternal pessimist, got the first part correct. There is a fine line in judgment and conscience. However, I think America and the healthcare industry have uniformly failed at allowing our collective conscience to be our guide. It is not erroneous, but deeply entrenched and consistent with our humanity.

Conversely, Winston Churchill stated, "The only guide to a [people] is [their] conscience; the only shield to [their] memory is

EPILOGUE

the rectitude and sincerity of [their] actions."[2] He also wrote, "All the great things are simple, and many can be expressed in a single word: freedom, justice, honor, duty, mercy, hope."[3]

On some occasions, I have the joy and high honor to pray with my daughter before she goes to sleep. Prior to prayer, I work to discover her thoughts, fears, and philosophies on life within her ever-evolving adolescent brain. This is no small feat as she is a chip off the old block and does not open up easily, even to me. Regardless of how her day goes, I always wish her a good night and better tomorrows. It is the same thing I wish for America and the American health system: better tomorrows.

---

[1] *Leviathan*, by Thomas Hobbes (East India Publishing Company, 2021); pages 213-214.
[2] Speech on Neville Chamberlain in the House of Commons, by Winston Churchill (November 12, 1940).
[3] *If I Lived My Life Again*, by Winston Churchill (W. H. Allen, 1974).

www.ingramcontent.com/pod-product-compliance
Lightning Source LLC
Chambersburg PA
CBHW020425010526
44118CB00010B/425